Table of Contents

Chapter 1 Introduction to Generative AI 6
    Overview of Generative AI 6
        Historical Background and Evolution 6
        Applications and Use Cases 7
        How Generative AI Works 7
        Challenges and Limitations 8
        Future Directions 8
    Overview of Generative Adversarial Networks (GANs) 10
History and Evolution of Generative Models 10
Applications of Generative AI in Various Fields 11
Chapter 2 Fundamentals of Deep Learning 15
    Basics of Neural Networks 15
    Training and Optimization Techniques 17
    Convolutional Neural Networks (CNNs) and Recurrent Neural Networks (RNNs) 19
    Introduction to Autoencoders 21
Chapter 3   Generative Adversarial Networks (GANs) 24
    Architecture and Components of GANs 24
Training GANs: Adversarial Training Process 26
Variants of GANs 29
Challenges and Limitations of GANs 31
Chapter 4   Variational Autoencoders (VAEs) 35

Introduction to Variational Inference 35

Architecture and Training of VAEs 37

Latent Space Representation and Sampling 40

Applications of VAEs in Image Generation and Representation Learning 42

> Basic Python code snippet demonstrating how to use Variational Autoencoders (VAEs) for image generation and representation learning using TensorFlow and Keras: .. 44

Chapter 5   Generative Models for Text and Language 48

Recurrent Neural Networks (RNNs) for Sequence Generation 48

> Basic Python code example demonstrating how to train a Recurrent Neural Network (RNN) for text generation using TensorFlow and Keras: 50

Long Short-Term Memory Networks (LSTMs) and Gated Recurrent Units (GRUs) 52

Transformers and Attention Mechanisms 54

Text Generation with GPT (Generative Pre-trained Transformer) Models 57

> Basic Python code example demonstrating how to generate text using a pre-trained GPT model from the Hugging Face Transformers library: 59

Chapter 6   Image Generation with GANs 62

StyleGAN and StyleGAN2: High-Quality Image Synthesis 62

> A simplified example using TensorFlow and the official StyleGAN2 implementation from NVlabs: 64

Conditional Image Generation 66

Implementing conditional image generation in Python 68

Image-to-Image Translation: Pix2Pix, CycleGAN, etc. 72

Implementing Pix2Pix for image-to-image translation in Python 74

Super-Resolution and Image Inpainting with GANs 77

> A simplified Python code example for implementing super-resolution and image inpainting using Generative Adversarial Networks (GANs) with TensorFlow: 79

Chapter 7   Generative Models for Music and Audio 82

WaveGAN and SpecGAN: Audio Synthesis 89
Voice Conversion and Speech Synthesis 94
Chapter-8   Ethical and Societal Implications of Generative AI 100
Deepfakes and Synthetic Media 100
Bias and Fairness in Generative Models 104
Regulation and Responsible Use of Generative AI 110
Chapter-9   Large Language Models (LLMs) 113
Fundamentals of Natural Language Processing (NLP) 116
Basics of NLP: Tokenization, Lemmatization, and Part-of-Speech Tagging 116
1. Tokenization 116
2. Lemmatization 117
Part-of-Speech (POS) Tagging: 119
Word Embeddings: Word2Vec, GloVe, and FastText .. 120
Word2Vec: 120
GloVe (Global Vectors for Word Representation): 122
FastText: 124
Variants of Transformers: BERT, GPT, T5, XLNet, etc. ... 126
Pre-training and Fine-tuning LLMs 137
Pre-training Objectives: Masked Language Modeling, Next Sentence Prediction 137
Training Procedure in LLM 142
Fine-tuning Strategies in LLM 158
Chapter-10   LLama (Large Language Model Meta AI) .. 178
LLama 178
Creating a chatbot using the LLama model 182
Natural Language Understanding using LLAMA 185
Comparing LLama with other Large Language Models (LLMs) 188
Chapter-11   Prompt Engineering 191
Prompt Engineering 191
Setting Up Your Environment 194

Techniques for Effective Prompt Design 219
  Prompt Templates 219
  Few-Shot and Zero-Shot Learning 222
    Few-Shot Learning with Prototypical Networks (PyTorch): 224
    Zero-Shot Learning with Semantic Embeddings (TensorFlow): ... 225
  Applications of Prompt Engineering 227
    Chatbots and Virtual Assistants Using Prompt Engineering 227
    Example: Building a Simple Chatbot with GPT-3.5 227
    Advanced Prompt Engineering Techniques 230
  Content Creation Tools 231
    Example: Creating a Blog Post Generator 232
    Advanced Content Creation Techniques 233
  Interactive AI Systems 235
    Example: Building an Interactive AI System 236
    Advanced Interactive AI Techniques 238
Chapter 12   Retrieval-Augmented Generation (RAG) Framework ... 240
  Retrieval-Augmented Generation (RAG) Framework 240
    How RAG Works 241
    Example: Implementing a Simple RAG System 242
  Components of the Retrieval-Augmented Generation (RAG) Framework ... 245
    Example: Implementing a Simple RAG System with Components ... 246
  Working Mechanism of Retrieval-Augmented Generation (RAG) 249
  Implementing RAG in AI Systems 254
Chapter 13   Future Directions and Emerging Trends ... 261
  Advances in Generative AI Research 263
  Challenges and Opportunities in the Field 265
  Potential Applications and Impact on Society 267

Chapter 14   Resources and Further Reading 270
    Books: 270
    Online Courses: 270
    Research Papers: 270
    Websites and Blogs: 271
    Online Communities: 271
    Conferences and Workshops: 271

Chapter 1 Introduction to Generative AI

Overview of Generative AI

Generative AI refers to a class of artificial intelligence models designed to generate new content, such as text, images, music, and even video, based on the data they have been trained on. Unlike traditional AI models that are typically used for classification, prediction, or analysis, generative AI models create new data instances that are similar to the training data.
Historical Background and Evolution

Generative AI has its roots in early AI research on neural networks and machine learning. Key milestones in its development include:

- **1960s-1970s:** Initial experiments with simple generative algorithms, such as rule-based systems and early neural networks.

- **1980s-1990s:** Development of more sophisticated neural networks and the introduction of genetic algorithms.

- **2000s:** The rise of deep learning, with significant advancements in neural network architectures.

- **2014:** Introduction of Generative Adversarial Networks (GANs) by Ian Goodfellow and colleagues, which significantly boosted the field of generative modeling.

- **2018:** The debut of Transformer models, particularly OpenAI's GPT (Generative Pre-trained Transformer), which revolutionized text generation tasks.

- **2020s:** Continued advancements with models like GPT-3 and DALL-E, leading to more powerful and versatile generative AI applications.

Applications and Use Cases

Generative AI is used across various industries for a wide range of applications:

- **Text Generation:** Creating articles, poetry, chatbots, and code completion (e.g., GPT-3).

- **Image Generation:** Producing realistic images from descriptions, style transfer, and enhancing image quality (e.g., DALL-E, GANs).

- **Music and Audio:** Composing music, generating sound effects, and synthesizing voices (e.g., OpenAI's Jukebox).

- **Video and Animation:** Generating video content, deepfakes, and enhancing video quality.

- **Design and Art:** Assisting artists and designers by generating new designs and artwork.

- **Healthcare:** Drug discovery, generating synthetic medical data for research, and creating educational materials.

- **Gaming and Virtual Worlds:** Creating characters, landscapes, and scenarios in video games.

How Generative AI Works

Generative AI models are typically based on deep learning architectures, such as:

- **Generative Adversarial Networks (GANs):** Consist of two neural networks, a generator and a discriminator, that are trained together in a competitive process to create realistic data.

- **Variational Autoencoders (VAEs):** Use probabilistic methods to generate new data points by encoding input data into a latent space and then decoding it.

- **Transformer Models:** Utilize self-attention mechanisms to generate coherent sequences of text, images, or other data types.

These models learn the underlying patterns and structures in the training data and use this knowledge to produce new, similar data. The training process involves optimizing the model's parameters to minimize the difference between the generated data and the real data.

Challenges and Limitations

While generative AI holds great promise, it also faces several challenges:

- **Quality Control:** Ensuring the generated content is accurate and high-quality.

- **Ethics and Bias:** Addressing biases present in the training data to avoid generating harmful or biased content.

- **Computational Resources:** Training and deploying generative models require significant computational power.

- **Misuse:** Potential for misuse in creating deepfakes, misinformation, and other harmful content.

Future Directions

Generative AI continues to evolve, with ongoing research aimed at:

- **Improving Model Efficiency:** Developing more efficient architectures and training techniques.

- **Enhancing Creativity:** Enabling models to generate more diverse and creative outputs.

- **Ethical AI:** Creating frameworks and guidelines to ensure ethical use and reduce biases.

- **Interdisciplinary Applications:** Expanding the use of generative AI into new fields and integrating it with other technologies like augmented reality (AR) and virtual reality (VR).

Generative AI is a transformative technology with the potential to revolutionize many aspects of society, from creative arts to scientific research, by enabling machines to generate content that was previously the domain of human creativity.

Overview of Generative Adversarial Networks (GANs)

In the world of artificial intelligence and machine learning, Generative Adversarial Networks (GANs) stand out as a revolutionary concept. These networks consist of two neural networks, the generator and the discriminator, which work in tandem to generate new data samples that mimic the distribution of the training data.

In this chapter, we'll delve into the fundamentals of GANs, exploring their architecture, training process, and applications across various domains. From generating realistic images and videos to creating synthetic text and music, GANs have unlocked endless possibilities in the field of generative modelling.

Through clear explanations and illustrative examples, we'll uncover the inner workings of GANs and showcase their potential to push the boundaries of creativity and innovation in artificial intelligence. Whether you're a seasoned researcher or a curious beginner, this chapter will provide a comprehensive overview of GANs and their impact on the future of machine learning.

History and Evolution of Generative Models

The history and evolution of Generative Adversarial Networks (GANs) trace back to the early 2010s when Ian Goodfellow and his colleagues introduced the concept in their seminal paper published in 2014. However, the roots of generative modeling can be found in earlier works dating back to the 1980s and 1990s.

In this chapter, we'll explore the historical timeline of generative models, starting from the early attempts to model probability distributions to the breakthroughs that led to the development of GANs. We'll delve into key milestones and influential works in the field, including Boltzmann machines, Restricted Boltzmann Machines (RBMs), Variational Autoencoders (VAEs), and Deep Belief Networks (DBNs).

We'll also examine the challenges and limitations of early generative models and how GANs addressed many of these issues by introducing a novel adversarial training framework. By pitting a generator against a discriminator in a game-theoretic setting, GANs revolutionized the field of generative modelling and paved the way for unprecedented advancements in artificial intelligence.

Through a comprehensive exploration of the history and evolution of generative models, this chapter aims to provide readers with a deeper understanding of the context in which GANs emerged and the transformative impact they have had on the field of machine learning.

Applications of Generative AI in Various Fields

Generative Artificial Intelligence (AI) has found applications across various domains, revolutionizing industries and unlocking new possibilities in creativity, innovation, and problem-solving. In this chapter, we'll explore some of the diverse applications of Generative AI and their impact on different fields:

1. **Image Synthesis and Enhancement**: Generative models like Generative Adversarial Networks (GANs) have been widely used for image synthesis and enhancement tasks. They can generate realistic images of people, objects, and scenes, enabling applications in virtual reality, gaming, and content creation.

2. **Art and Design**: Generative AI has empowered artists and designers to explore new creative avenues by generating novel artworks, designs, and visual concepts. Artists use generative models to create unique digital art pieces, generate patterns, and explore artistic styles.

3. **Medical Imaging and Diagnosis**: Generative models are being leveraged to generate synthetic medical images for training and validating imaging algorithms. They also aid in medical image enhancement, segmentation, and disease diagnosis, helping medical professionals make more accurate and timely diagnoses.

4. **Natural Language Generation**: In the field of natural language processing (NLP), Generative AI is used for text generation, dialogue systems, and language translation. Models like OpenAI's GPT series can generate coherent and contextually relevant text, enabling applications in chatbots, content generation, and language understanding.

5. **Drug Discovery and Molecular Design**: Generative models play a crucial role in drug discovery and molecular design by generating novel chemical compounds with desired properties. They facilitate virtual screening of compounds, de novo drug design, and optimization of molecular structures, accelerating the drug development process.

6. **Music Composition and Audio Synthesis**: Generative AI techniques are employed in music composition and audio synthesis to generate novel musical compositions, soundtracks, and audio effects. These models can mimic different musical styles, create harmonious melodies, and even generate entire music tracks autonomously.

7. **Fashion and Apparel Design**: Generative models are transforming the fashion industry by generating new clothing designs, patterns, and styles. Fashion designers use AI-powered tools to explore creative possibilities, personalize designs, and optimize garment production processes.

8. **Data Augmentation and Synthetic Data Generation**: Generative AI is utilized for data augmentation and synthetic data generation in machine learning applications. These models can generate realistic synthetic data samples to supplement training datasets, improve model robustness, and address data scarcity issues.

9. **Environmental Simulation and Modelling**: Generative models are employed in environmental simulation and modelling to generate realistic simulations of natural phenomena, climate patterns, and ecological systems. These simulations aid researchers and policymakers in understanding

complex environmental dynamics and making informed decisions.

Content Generation and Personalization: Generative AI powers content generation and personalization platforms, creating tailored experiences for users across various digital platforms. These models generate personalized recommendations, product descriptions, and marketing content based on user preferences and behaviour.

Through these diverse applications, Generative AI is reshaping industries, driving innovation, and unlocking new opportunities for creativity and problem-solving. As the field continues to advance, we can expect to see even more impactful applications emerge, transforming the way we live, work, and interact with technology.

Chapter 2
Fundamentals of Deep Learning

Basics of Neural Networks

In this chapter, we'll explore the basics of neural networks, which serve as the foundation for many advanced machine learning and artificial intelligence techniques. We'll cover key concepts, architectures, and training algorithms, providing a solid understanding of how neural networks work.

1. **Introduction to Neural Networks**:
    - Definition and Overview: What are neural networks and how do they mimic the human brain?
    - Historical Background: Evolution of neural network models from the perceptron to deep learning.

2. **Neuron Model**:
    - Structure of Neurons: Anatomy and function of biological neurons.
    - Artificial Neurons: Mathematical representation and activation functions.

3. **Feedforward Neural Networks**:
    - Architecture: Layers, neurons, and connections in a feedforward neural network.
    - Forward Propagation: How inputs are processed through the network to produce outputs.
    - Activation Functions: Common activation functions like sigmoid, tanh, and ReLU.

4. **Training Neural Networks:**
    - Loss Functions: Objective functions used to measure the network's performance.
    - Backpropagation: Algorithm for updating network weights to minimize loss.
    - Gradient Descent: Optimization technique used to find the minimum of the loss function.

5. **Deep Learning Architectures:**
    - Multilayer Perceptrons (MLPs): Basic feedforward neural networks with multiple layers.
    - Convolutional Neural Networks (CNNs): Specialized for image recognition and computer vision tasks.
    - Recurrent Neural Networks (RNNs): Designed for sequential data and time-series analysis.

6. **Regularization and Optimization:**
    - Overfitting and Underfitting: Challenges in training neural networks and techniques to mitigate them.
    - Dropout: Regularization technique to prevent overfitting by randomly dropping neurons during training.
    - Batch Normalization: Technique to improve the stability and performance of deep neural networks.

7. **Hyperparameter Tuning:**
    - Learning Rate: Key hyperparameter that controls the step size during gradient descent.
    - Batch Size and Epochs: Parameters that affect the speed and convergence of training.
    - Number of Layers and Neurons: Architecture choices that impact the network's capacity and expressiveness.

8. **Applications of Neural Networks:**
    - Image Classification: Using CNNs for tasks like object recognition and image tagging.
    - Natural Language Processing: Applications of RNNs and transformers for text generation and sentiment analysis.
    - Reinforcement Learning: Integration of neural networks with reinforcement learning algorithms for game playing and robotics.

By the end of this section, readers will have a solid understanding of the fundamentals of neural networks and their applications across various domains. They will be well-equipped to dive deeper into advanced topics in deep learning and artificial intelligence.

Training and Optimization Techniques

In this section, we'll delve into the training and optimization techniques used in machine learning and deep learning models. These techniques are essential for achieving optimal performance, improving model convergence, and avoiding common pitfalls such as overfitting and underfitting. Let's explore some of the key training and optimization techniques:

1. **Gradient Descent**:
    - Overview: Gradient descent is a fundamental optimization algorithm used to minimize the loss function of a model.
    - Batch Gradient Descent: Update the model parameters based on the average gradient of the entire training dataset.
    - Stochastic Gradient Descent (SGD): Update the parameters based on the gradient of a single randomly selected training example.
    - Mini-batch Gradient Descent: Update the parameters based on the gradient of a small subset (mini-batch) of the training dataset.

2. **Learning Rate Scheduling**:
    - Fixed Learning Rate: Keep the learning rate constant throughout training.
    - Learning Rate Decay: Decrease the learning rate over time to fine-tune the model parameters.
    - Adaptive Learning Rate: Adjust the learning rate dynamically based on the model's performance or other factors.

3. **Regularization Techniques**:

- L1 and L2 Regularization: Add penalty terms to the loss function to discourage large weights.
- Dropout: Randomly deactivate neurons during training to prevent overfitting and promote model generalization.
- Early Stopping: Stop training when the performance on a validation dataset starts to degrade to prevent overfitting.

4. **Batch Normalization**:
   - Normalize the inputs to each layer of the model to speed up training and improve convergence.
   - Reduce the internal covariate shift by normalizing the activations between layers.

5. **Optimization Algorithms**:
   - Momentum Optimization: Incorporate the momentum term to accelerate convergence and dampen oscillations.
   - RMSprop (Root Mean Square Propagation): Adaptively adjust the learning rates for each parameter based on their gradients.
   - Adam (Adaptive Moment Estimation): Combines momentum optimization and RMSprop to achieve faster convergence and better generalization.

6. **Hyperparameter Tuning**:
   - Grid Search: Systematically search through a predefined set of hyperparameters to find the optimal combination.
   - Random Search: Randomly sample hyperparameters from a predefined distribution to explore the hyperparameter space efficiently.
   - Bayesian Optimization: Use probabilistic models to guide the search for optimal hyperparameters based on past evaluations.

7. **Data Augmentation**:
   - Increase the size and diversity of the training dataset by applying transformations such as rotation, scaling, and flipping.
   - Reduce overfitting and improve model generalization by introducing variations in the input data.

8. **Transfer Learning**:
    - Fine-tune pre-trained models on a target task by leveraging the knowledge learned from a related source task or dataset.
    - Speed up training and improve performance, especially when training data is limited.

By understanding and applying these training and optimization techniques, practitioners can effectively train machine learning and deep learning models, achieve better performance, and overcome common challenges encountered during the training process.

Convolutional Neural Networks (CNNs) and Recurrent Neural Networks (RNNs)

In this section, we'll explore two powerful types of neural networks: Convolutional Neural Networks (CNNs) and Recurrent Neural Networks (RNNs). These architectures are widely used in various fields such as computer vision, natural language processing, and time-series analysis. Let's dive into their key concepts, architectures, and applications:

1. **Convolutional Neural Networks (CNNs)**:

    - Overview: CNNs are designed to process and analyse visual data, making them ideal for tasks like image classification, object detection, and image segmentation.

    - Architecture: CNNs consist of convolutional layers, pooling layers, and fully connected layers.

    - Convolutional Layers: Apply convolutional filters to extract features from input images.

- Pooling Layers: Reduce the spatial dimensions of feature maps while preserving important information.

- Fully Connected Layers: Flatten the feature maps and connect them to the output layer for classification or regression.

2. **Applications of CNNs:**

    - Image Classification: Classify objects and scenes in images with high accuracy.

    - Object Detection: Identify and localize objects within an image, often using techniques like region proposal networks (RPNs) and anchor boxes.

    - Image Segmentation: Segment images into meaningful regions or objects, enabling applications like medical image analysis and autonomous driving.

3. **Recurrent Neural Networks (RNNs):**

    - Overview: RNNs are designed to process sequential data with temporal dependencies, making them suitable for tasks like speech recognition, language modelling, and time-series prediction.

    - Architecture: RNNs consist of recurrent units with feedback connections that allow them to maintain a memory of past inputs.

    - Long Short-Term Memory (LSTM) Cells: Specialized RNN cells that address the vanishing gradient problem and capture long-term dependencies.

    - Gated Recurrent Units (GRUs): Simplified versions of LSTM cells with fewer parameters but similar capabilities.

4. **Applications of RNNs:**

- Natural Language Processing (NLP): Perform tasks like machine translation, text generation, and sentiment analysis.

- Speech Recognition: Convert spoken language into text, enabling applications like virtual assistants and voice-controlled devices.

- Time-Series Prediction: Forecast future values based on historical data, used in fields like finance, weather forecasting, and stock market analysis.

5. **Hybrid Architectures**:

    - CNN-RNN Hybrid Models: Combine the strengths of CNNs and RNNs to process both spatial and temporal information, enabling tasks like video analysis and action recognition.

    - Attention Mechanisms: Enhance the capabilities of RNNs by selectively focusing on relevant parts of input sequences, improving performance in tasks like machine translation and image captioning.

By understanding the principles and applications of CNNs and RNNs, practitioners can leverage these powerful neural network architectures to tackle a wide range of real-world problems in computer vision, natural language processing, and beyond.

Introduction to Autoencoders

Autoencoders are a class of neural networks primarily used for unsupervised learning tasks such as dimensionality reduction, data denoising, and feature extraction. In this chapter, we'll provide an introduction to autoencoders, exploring their architecture, training process, and various applications.

1. **Overview of Autoencoders**:

- Definition: Autoencoders are neural networks designed to learn efficient representations of input data by compressing it into a lower-dimensional latent space and then reconstructing the original data from this compressed representation.

- Purpose: Autoencoders are commonly used for tasks such as data compression, anomaly detection, and generative modeling.

2. **Architecture of Autoencoders:**

    - Encoder: The encoder network maps the input data to a lower-dimensional latent space, compressing the information.

    - Latent Space: The latent space represents a compressed, low-dimensional representation of the input data, capturing its essential features.

    - Decoder: The decoder network reconstructs the original data from the latent space representation, aiming to minimize the reconstruction error.

3. **Training Autoencoders:**

    - Objective Function: The training objective of autoencoders typically involves minimizing the reconstruction error between the input data and its reconstructed counterpart.

    - Loss Function: Common loss functions used for training autoencoders include mean squared error (MSE) and binary cross-entropy loss, depending on the nature of the input data.

    - Optimization: Autoencoders are trained using gradient-based optimization algorithms such as stochastic gradient descent (SGD) or its variants.

4. **Types of Autoencoders:**

    - Basic Autoencoder: The standard autoencoder architecture with a symmetric encoder and decoder.

- Variational Autoencoder (VAE): A probabilistic variant of autoencoders that learns a probabilistic distribution over the latent space, enabling generation of new data samples.

- Denoising Autoencoder: Autoencoders trained to reconstruct clean data from noisy input, helping in data denoising and feature extraction.

- Sparse Autoencoder: Autoencoders with regularization techniques to induce sparsity in the latent space representation, aiding in feature learning and interpretation.

5. **Applications of Autoencoders**:

- Dimensionality Reduction: Reduce the dimensionality of high-dimensional data while preserving its essential features.

- Data Denoising: Remove noise from corrupted data samples, enhancing the quality of the reconstructed data.

- Anomaly Detection: Identify unusual or anomalous patterns in data by comparing reconstruction errors.

- Generative Modeling: Generate new data samples by sampling from the learned latent space distribution, as demonstrated by Variational Autoencoders (VAEs).

By understanding the principles and applications of autoencoders, practitioners can leverage these versatile neural networks for a wide range of unsupervised learning tasks, enabling efficient representation learning and data-driven insights.

Chapter 3 Generative Adversarial Networks (GANs)

Architecture and Components of GANs

In this section, we'll explore the architecture and components of Generative Adversarial Networks (GANs), a powerful class of deep learning models used for generative tasks such as image generation, data synthesis, and creative applications.

1. **Overview of GANs**:

    - Definition: Generative Adversarial Networks (GANs) are a type of deep learning model consisting of two neural networks, the generator and the discriminator, which are trained simultaneously through an adversarial process.

    - Purpose: GANs are designed to generate synthetic data samples that are indistinguishable from real data, enabling applications in image synthesis, data augmentation, and creative content generation.

2. **Components of GANs**:

    - Generator: The generator network takes random noise as input and generates synthetic data samples (e.g., images) in the output space. It learns to map noise vectors to realistic data distributions through a series of convolutional or dense layers.

- Discriminator: The discriminator network acts as a binary classifier that distinguishes between real and fake data samples. It learns to differentiate between real data samples from the training dataset and synthetic samples generated by the generator.

- Adversarial Training: GANs are trained using an adversarial process where the generator and discriminator networks are pitted against each other. The generator aims to produce high-quality synthetic samples that can fool the discriminator, while the discriminator strives to accurately distinguish between real and fake samples.

3. **Training Process:**

    - Minimax Game: GAN training can be formulated as a minimax game, where the generator and discriminator networks play against each other to optimize their respective objectives. The generator aims to minimize the discriminator's ability to differentiate between real and fake samples, while the discriminator aims to maximize its accuracy.

    - Backpropagation and Gradient Descent: GANs are trained using backpropagation and gradient descent algorithms. The generator and discriminator networks are updated iteratively based on the gradients of their respective loss functions, which are typically adversarial in nature.

4. **Loss Functions:**

    - Generator Loss: The generator's objective is to minimize the discrepancy between the distributions of real and fake samples, typically measured using metrics such as binary cross-entropy or Wasserstein distance.

    - Discriminator Loss: The discriminator's objective is to accurately distinguish between real and fake samples, typically measured using binary cross-entropy loss or other classification loss functions.

5. **Variants of GANs**:

    - Conditional GANs: GANs that generate samples conditioned on additional input variables, such as class labels or attribute vectors.

    - Wasserstein GANs (WGANs): Variants of GANs that use Wasserstein distance as the training objective to stabilize training and improve sample quality.

    - Progressive GANs: GAN architectures that progressively grow in resolution during training, enabling the generation of high-quality images with fine details.

By understanding the architecture and components of GANs, practitioners can harness the power of generative adversarial networks for a wide range of applications in image synthesis, data augmentation, and creative content generation.

Training GANs: Adversarial Training Process

In this chapter, we'll delve into the training process of Generative Adversarial Networks (GANs), focusing on the adversarial training paradigm that underpins their operation.

Understanding the intricacies of GAN training is crucial for achieving stable convergence and generating high-quality synthetic data. Let's explore the adversarial training process of GANs:

1. **Adversarial Training Paradigm**:

    - Concept: GANs are trained using an adversarial process where two neural networks, the generator and the discriminator, are trained simultaneously through competition. The generator aims to produce synthetic data samples that are indistinguishable from real data, while the discriminator learns to differentiate between real and fake samples.

    - Minimax Game: GAN training can be formulated as a minimax game between the generator and the discriminator. The generator's objective is to minimize the discriminator's ability to distinguish between real and fake samples, while the discriminator's objective is to maximize its accuracy in classifying real and fake samples.

2. **Training Workflow**:

    - Initialization: Initialize the weights of the generator and discriminator networks with random values.

    - Forward Pass: Generate synthetic data samples using the generator and pass them through the discriminator to obtain predictions.

    - Calculation of Loss: Compute the loss functions for both the generator and discriminator based on their respective objectives.

    - Backpropagation: Update the parameters of the generator and discriminator networks using gradient descent optimization algorithms. The gradients are backpropagated through the networks to adjust the weights and minimize the loss functions.

- Adversarial Training: Iterate between updating the parameters of the generator and discriminator networks in an adversarial manner, allowing them to learn from each other's mistakes and improve their performance over time.

3. **Generator Loss Function**:

    - Objective: The generator aims to minimize the discrepancy between the distributions of real and fake samples, encouraging the generation of realistic synthetic data.

    - Loss Metrics: Common loss functions used for the generator include binary cross-entropy loss, Wasserstein distance, or other divergence measures.

4. **Discriminator Loss Function**:

    - Objective: The discriminator aims to accurately differentiate between real and fake samples, helping to guide the training of the generator.

    - Loss Metrics: The discriminator's loss function typically involves binary cross-entropy loss or other classification loss functions.

5. **Training Challenges and Techniques**:

    - Mode Collapse: Occurs when the generator learns to produce a limited set of samples, ignoring the diversity of the training data. Techniques such as mini-batch discrimination and diversity-promoting objectives can help alleviate mode collapse.

    - Gradient Vanishing and Exploding: Challenges related to gradient instability during training can be addressed using techniques such as gradient clipping, weight initialization strategies, and alternative loss functions (e.g., Wasserstein distance).

    By understanding the adversarial training process of GANs and the associated challenges and techniques, practitioners can effectively train GAN models to generate high-quality synthetic data for a wide range of applications in image synthesis, data augmentation, and creative content generation.

Variants of GANs

In this section, we'll explore various variants of Generative Adversarial Networks (GANs), each with unique architectures, training objectives, and applications. These GAN variants extend the capabilities of traditional GANs and address specific challenges encountered during training. Let's delve into some of the most prominent variants:

1. **Conditional GANs (cGANs):**

   Overview: Conditional GANs extend the basic GAN architecture by conditioning both the generator and discriminator networks on additional input variables, such as class labels, attributes, or context information.
   Architecture: In cGANs, the generator takes both random noise and conditioning information as input to generate conditional samples, while the discriminator receives both real data samples and conditioning information for classification.
   Applications: cGANs are widely used for conditional image generation tasks such as image-to-image translation, text-to-image synthesis, and semantic image editing.

2. **Wasserstein GANs (WGANs):**

   - Overview: WGANs introduce Wasserstein distance (also known as Earth Mover's distance) as a more stable training objective compared to the traditional minimax game formulation used in standard GANs.

- Training Objective: Instead of minimizing the Jensen-Shannon divergence or Kullback-Leibler divergence between real and fake distributions, WGANs aim to minimize the Wasserstein distance, which provides a smoother and more meaningful measure of distributional discrepancy.

- Benefits: WGANs often exhibit improved stability during training, mitigating issues such as mode collapse and gradient instability commonly observed in traditional GANs.

- Applications: WGANs have been successfully applied to various generative tasks, including image synthesis, data augmentation, and generative modeling.

3. **Progressive GANs:**

    - Overview: Progressive GANs are designed to generate high-resolution images with fine details by progressively growing the resolution of both the generator and discriminator networks during training.

    - Training Strategy: Progressive GANs start with low-resolution images and gradually increase the resolution over multiple training iterations, adding new layers and feature maps to both networks.

    - Benefits: Progressive GANs enable the generation of high-quality images with intricate details, such as those found in natural photographs or artistic paintings.

    - Applications: Progressive GANs are commonly used in applications requiring high-resolution image synthesis, such as image editing, super-resolution, and digital art generation.

4. **StyleGAN and StyleGAN2:**

    - Overview: StyleGAN and its successor, StyleGAN2, introduce style-based architecture and adaptive instance normalization (AdaIN) layers to generate high-quality and diverse images with controllable visual attributes.

- Architecture: StyleGAN models separate the latent space into style and content representations, allowing for fine-grained control over various visual attributes such as pose, expression, and hairstyle.

- Applications: StyleGAN and StyleGAN2 have been widely used in applications such as face generation, artistic image synthesis, and deepfake generation.

By exploring these variants of GANs, practitioners can leverage their unique architectures and training objectives to tackle a wide range of generative tasks and challenges in computer vision, natural language processing, and creative content generation.

Challenges and Limitations of GANs

In this section, we'll explore the challenges and limitations associated with Generative Adversarial Networks (GANs), despite their remarkable success in various generative tasks. Understanding these challenges is essential for practitioners to effectively deploy GAN models and mitigate potential issues. Let's delve into some of the key challenges and limitations of GANs:

1. **Mode Collapse**:

    - Description: Mode collapse occurs when the generator learns to produce a limited set of samples, ignoring the diversity present in the training data distribution.

- Cause: Mode collapse can be caused by imbalanced training dynamics, where the generator exploits weaknesses in the discriminator without effectively covering the entire data space.

- Mitigation Strategies: Techniques such as mini-batch discrimination, diversity-promoting objectives, and architectural modifications can help mitigate mode collapse and encourage the generation of diverse samples.

2. **Gradient Instability**:

    - Description: GAN training is susceptible to issues related to gradient vanishing and exploding, especially in the early stages of training or when the discriminator becomes too dominant.

    - Cause: Gradient instability arises from the non-convex nature of the GAN objective function, leading to vanishing or exploding gradients during backpropagation.

    - Mitigation Strategies: Techniques such as gradient clipping, weight normalization, spectral normalization, and alternative loss functions (e.g., Wasserstein distance) can help stabilize GAN training and mitigate gradient instability.

3. **Evaluation and Metrics**:

    - Description: Evaluating the performance of GANs and comparing different models can be challenging due to the lack of objective metrics that accurately capture the quality, diversity, and realism of generated samples.

    - Cause: Traditional evaluation metrics such as Inception Score (IS) and Frechet Inception Distance (FID) have limitations and may not always correlate with human perceptual judgments.

- Mitigation Strategies: Researchers are actively exploring new evaluation metrics and methodologies that better align with human perception, such as human evaluation studies, perceptual similarity metrics, and generative quality assessment models.

4. **Training Instability**:

    - Description: GAN training can be highly sensitive to hyperparameters, initialization schemes, and architectural choices, leading to training instability and suboptimal convergence.

    - Cause: Factors such as learning rate schedules, batch size, network depth, and activation functions can significantly impact the stability and convergence of GAN training.

    - Mitigation Strategies: Employing careful hyperparameter tuning, regularization techniques, progressive training strategies, and early stopping criteria can help stabilize GAN training and improve convergence.

5. **Robustness to Distribution Shifts**:

    - Description: GANs trained on a specific dataset may lack robustness when applied to data distributions that differ significantly from the training distribution.

    - Cause: GANs may overfit to the specific characteristics of the training data distribution, making them less effective at generalizing to unseen data distributions.

    - Mitigation Strategies: Techniques such as domain adaptation, domain randomization, and fine-tuning on target domain data can help improve the robustness of GAN models to distribution shifts.

By acknowledging and addressing these challenges and limitations, practitioners can enhance the robustness, stability, and effectiveness of GAN models for various generative tasks and applications in computer vision, natural language processing, and beyond.

Chapter 4 Variational Autoencoders (VAEs)

Introduction to Variational Inference

In this chapter, we'll introduce the concept of Variational Inference, a powerful technique used in Bayesian statistics and machine learning to approximate complex posterior distributions. Variational Inference offers an efficient and scalable approach for Bayesian inference, especially in high-dimensional and large-scale datasets. Let's explore the key concepts and principles of Variational Inference:

1. **Bayesian Inference**:

    - Overview: Bayesian inference is a framework for probabilistic reasoning that involves updating beliefs about uncertain parameters based on observed data.

    - Posterior Distribution: In Bayesian inference, the goal is to compute the posterior distribution of model parameters given the observed data, which quantifies our updated beliefs about the parameters after observing the data.

    - Challenges: Computing the exact posterior distribution can be analytically intractable, especially for complex models with high-dimensional parameter spaces.

2. **Variational Inference (VI)**:

- Motivation: Variational Inference offers a practical and scalable approach to approximate complex posterior distributions by framing the problem as an optimization task.

- Variational Distribution: VI introduces a family of parameterized distributions, known as the variational distribution or variational posterior, which serves as an approximation to the true posterior distribution.

- Optimization Objective: The goal of VI is to find the variational distribution that minimizes the Kullback-Leibler (KL) divergence from the true posterior distribution. Minimizing the KL divergence ensures that the variational approximation closely matches the true posterior distribution.

3. **Mean Field Variational Inference:**

    - Simplified Approach: Mean Field Variational Inference is a commonly used technique that simplifies the variational distribution by assuming that the variables are independent and factorized.
    - Factorization Assumption: Under the mean field assumption, the variational distribution factorizes into independent distributions for each latent variable, making the optimization tractable.

    - Coordinate Ascent Optimization: Mean Field VI typically involves iterative updates to each parameter of the variational distribution, often using coordinate ascent or gradient-based optimization techniques.

4. **Optimization Algorithms:**

    - Expectation-Maximization (EM) Algorithm: Variational Inference can be viewed as a generalization of the EM algorithm, where the E-step corresponds to computing the variational posterior and the M-step involves optimizing the variational parameters.

    - Stochastic Variational Inference (SVI): SVI extends VI to large-scale datasets by using stochastic optimization algorithms such as stochastic gradient descent (SGD) or its variants.

5. **Applications and Advantages**:

- Scalability: Variational Inference offers a scalable approach to Bayesian inference, making it suitable for large-scale datasets and complex models.

- Flexibility: VI provides flexibility in choosing the form of the variational distribution, allowing practitioners to tailor the approximation to the specific characteristics of the model and data.

- Approximate Inference: While Variational Inference may introduce approximation errors, it provides a trade-off between computational efficiency and accuracy, enabling practical Bayesian inference in real-world applications.

By understanding the principles and techniques of Variational Inference, practitioners can leverage this powerful tool for Bayesian inference in various machine learning tasks, including probabilistic modeling, latent variable modeling, and Bayesian deep learning.

Architecture and Training of VAEs

In this section, we'll delve into the architecture and training process of Variational Autoencoders (VAEs), a class of generative models that combine elements of autoencoders and variational inference. VAEs are widely used for unsupervised learning, data generation, and representation learning tasks. Let's explore the key components and principles of VAEs:

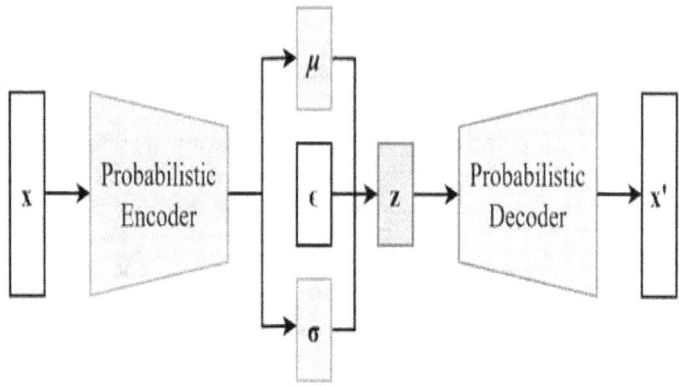

1. Overview of Variational Autoencoders (VAEs):

- Definition: Variational Autoencoders are generative models that aim to learn a low-dimensional latent representation of input data while simultaneously generating new data samples.

- Encoder-Decoder Architecture: VAEs consist of an encoder network, which maps input data to a latent space, and a decoder network, which reconstructs input data from latent variables.

- Variational Inference: VAEs employ variational inference to learn an approximate posterior distribution over latent variables, enabling efficient and scalable training.

2. Architecture of VAEs:

- Encoder Network: The encoder network takes input data and maps it to a distribution over latent variables. It typically consists of multiple layers of neural network units, such as convolutional or fully connected layers.

- Latent Space: The latent space represents a low-dimensional embedding of the input data, capturing meaningful features and structure. The encoder learns to map input data to the mean and variance parameters of the latent distribution.

- Reparameterization Trick: To enable backpropagation through the stochastic sampling process, VAEs use the reparameterization trick, which involves sampling latent variables from a factorized Gaussian distribution parameterized by the encoder outputs.

3. **Variational Objective Function**:

    - Objective Function: The training objective of VAEs consists of two components: a reconstruction loss, which measures the fidelity of the reconstructed data, and a regularization term, which encourages the latent distribution to approximate a prior distribution (usually a standard Gaussian).

    - Evidence Lower Bound (ELBO): The objective function of VAEs is often formulated as maximizing the Evidence Lower Bound (ELBO), which provides a lower bound on the log likelihood of the data under the true data distribution.

4. **Training Process**:

    - Stochastic Gradient Descent (SGD): VAEs are typically trained using SGD or its variants, such as Adam or RMSprop, to optimize the parameters of the encoder and decoder networks.

    - Reparameterization Gradient: During backpropagation, gradients are propagated through the encoder and decoder networks using the reparameterization trick, enabling end-to-end training of the VAE model.

    - Monte Carlo Estimation: Monte Carlo sampling is used to estimate the gradients of the ELBO with respect to the encoder parameters, allowing for efficient gradient-based optimization.

5. **Applications and Extensions**:

- Data Generation: VAEs can generate new data samples by sampling from the learned latent space and decoding them using the decoder network.

- Representation Learning: VAEs learn disentangled representations of input data, making them useful for tasks such as clustering, classification, and anomaly detection.

- Conditional VAEs: Extensions of VAEs, such as Conditional VAEs, allow for conditional generation of data samples conditioned on additional input variables, such as class labels or attributes.

By understanding the architecture and training process of VAEs, practitioners can leverage these powerful models for a wide range of applications in unsupervised learning, data generation, and representation learning.

Latent Space Representation and Sampling

Latent space representation plays a crucial role in VAEs by capturing meaningful features and structure of the input data in a lower-dimensional space. Let's explore the key concepts and techniques related to latent space representation and sampling:

1. Latent Space Representation:

- Definition: The latent space of a VAE represents a low-dimensional embedding of the input data, where each point corresponds to a different configuration of latent variables.

- Dimensionality Reduction: The latent space serves as a compressed representation of the input data, capturing the essential features and patterns in a lower-dimensional form.

- Continuous and Smooth: In ideal cases, the latent space of a VAE exhibits continuous and smooth transitions, allowing for meaningful interpolation and exploration of data variations.

2. Latent Space Encoding:

- Encoder Output: The encoder network of a VAE maps input data to a distribution over latent variables, typically parameterized by the mean and variance.

- Latent Distribution: The encoder output defines a multivariate Gaussian distribution in the latent space, characterized by its mean vector and covariance matrix.

- Sampling: Latent variables are sampled from the learned distribution using the reparameterization trick, enabling stochasticity during training and inference.

3. Latent Space Sampling:

- Random Sampling: In VAEs, new data samples can be generated by sampling latent variables from a prior distribution (e.g., standard Gaussian) and decoding them using the decoder network.

- Interpolation: Latent space interpolation involves traversing between two points in the latent space and generating intermediate data samples along the interpolated path.

- Exploration: Sampling from different regions of the latent space allows for the exploration of diverse data variations and generation of novel data samples.

4. Disentangled Representations:

- Disentanglement: VAEs aim to learn disentangled representations in the latent space, where each dimension corresponds to a semantically meaningful attribute or feature.

- Interpretability: Disentangled representations facilitate the interpretation and manipulation of specific attributes or features in generated data samples.

- Challenges: Achieving perfect disentanglement is challenging and often requires careful design choices, regularization techniques, and additional architectural modifications.

5. **Applications and Visualization**:

    - Data Generation: Latent space sampling enables the generation of new data samples with desired attributes or characteristics, such as style transfer, image morphing, and creative content generation.

    - Visualization: Techniques such as t-SNE (t-distributed stochastic neighbour embedding) or PCA (principal component analysis) can be used to visualize the latent space and explore the relationships between different data points.

By understanding latent space representation and sampling in VAEs, practitioners can leverage these techniques for data generation, exploration, and manipulation in various applications, including image synthesis, text generation, and creative AI.

Applications of VAEs in Image Generation and Representation Learning

Variational Autoencoders (VAEs) have found widespread applications in image generation and representation learning due to their ability to learn compact and structured latent representations of high-dimensional data. In this chapter, we'll explore some of the key applications of VAEs in image generation and representation learning:

1. **Image Generation**:
   - **Generative Modeling**: VAEs can generate realistic images by sampling from the learned latent space and decoding latent variables into image data.

   - **Variational Image Synthesis**: VAEs enable the synthesis of new images with desired attributes or styles by manipulating latent variables or conditioning on specific input features.

   - **Creative Content Generation**: VAEs can be used to create novel and artistic content, such as paintings, illustrations, and digital artwork, by exploring the latent space and sampling diverse data variations.

2. **Representation Learning**:
   - **Feature Extraction**: VAEs learn rich and informative representations of input images in the latent space, capturing important visual features and patterns.

   - **Disentangled Representations**: VAEs aim to learn disentangled representations, where each dimension of the latent space corresponds to a semantically meaningful attribute or feature.

   - **Transfer Learning**: Pre-trained VAEs can be used as feature extractors for downstream tasks such as classification, segmentation, and object detection, leveraging the learned representations for improved performance on target tasks.

3. **Image Reconstruction and Denoising**:
   - **Reconstruction**: VAEs reconstruct input images from their latent representations, enabling image reconstruction and denoising by removing noise or imperfections from the original images.

- **Anomaly Detection**: Deviations between reconstructed and original images can be used for anomaly detection and outlier identification in image data, facilitating quality control and defect detection in manufacturing and medical imaging applications.

4. **Data Augmentation and Style Transfer**:

    - **Data Augmentation**: VAEs can generate augmented data samples by perturbing latent representations or introducing variations in the latent space, augmenting the training dataset and improving model generalization.

    - **Style Transfer**: By manipulating latent variables corresponding to style attributes, VAEs enable style transfer between images, allowing for artistic transformations and creative visual effects.

5. **Semantic Image Editing and Manipulation**:

    - **Semantic Editing**: VAEs enable semantic image editing by selectively modifying latent variables associated with specific attributes or features, such as colors, shapes, and textures.

    - **Attribute Manipulation**: VAEs allow for attribute manipulation in images, such as changing facial expressions, hair styles, or background scenes, while preserving other image content.

By leveraging VAEs in image generation and representation learning, practitioners can harness the power of generative models to create, manipulate, and understand visual content in diverse domains, ranging from computer vision and graphics to creative arts and entertainment.

Basic Python code snippet demonstrating how to use Variational Autoencoders (VAEs) for image generation and representation learning using TensorFlow and Keras:

```python
import numpy as np
import matplotlib.pyplot as plt
import tensorflow as tf
from tensorflow import keras
from tensorflow.keras import layers

# Define VAE architecture
latent_dim = 2

# Encoder
encoder_inputs = keras.Input(shape=(28, 28, 1))
x = layers.Conv2D(32, 3, activation='relu', strides=2, padding='same')(encoder_inputs)
x = layers.Conv2D(64, 3, activation='relu', strides=2, padding='same')(x)
x = layers.Flatten()(x)
z_mean = layers.Dense(latent_dim, name='z_mean')(x)
z_log_var = layers.Dense(latent_dim, name='z_log_var')(x)

# Reparameterization trick
def sampling(args):
    z_mean, z_log_var = args
    epsilon = tf.random.normal(shape=(tf.shape(z_mean)[0], latent_dim), mean=0., stddev=1.)
    return z_mean + tf.exp(0.5 * z_log_var) * epsilon

z = layers.Lambda(sampling, output_shape=(latent_dim,), name='z')([z_mean, z_log_var])

# Decoder
latent_inputs = keras.Input(shape=(latent_dim,))
x = layers.Dense(7 * 7 * 64, activation='relu')(latent_inputs)
x = layers.Reshape((7, 7, 64))(x)
x = layers.Conv2DTranspose(64, 3, activation='relu', strides=2, padding='same')(x)
x = layers.Conv2DTranspose(32, 3, activation='relu', strides=2, padding='same')(x)
decoder_outputs = layers.Conv2DTranspose(1, 3, activation='sigmoid', padding='same')(x)

# Define VAE model
encoder = keras.Model(encoder_inputs, [z_mean, z_log_var, z], name='encoder')
decoder = keras.Model(latent_inputs, decoder_outputs, name='decoder')
```

```python
vae_outputs = decoder(encoder(encoder_inputs)[2])
vae = keras.Model(encoder_inputs, vae_outputs, name='vae')

# Define loss function
reconstruction_loss = keras.losses.mse(encoder_inputs, vae_outputs)
reconstruction_loss *= 28 * 28
kl_loss = 1 + z_log_var - tf.square(z_mean) - tf.exp(z_log_var)
kl_loss = tf.reduce_mean(kl_loss)
kl_loss *= -0.5
vae_loss = tf.reduce_mean(reconstruction_loss + kl_loss)
vae.add_loss(vae_loss)
vae.compile(optimizer='adam')

# Load and preprocess MNIST dataset
(x_train, _), (x_test, _) = keras.datasets.mnist.load_data()
x_train = x_train.astype('float32') / 255.
x_test = x_test.astype('float32') / 255.
x_train = np.expand_dims(x_train, -1)
x_test = np.expand_dims(x_test, -1)

# Train VAE
vae.fit(x_train, x_train, epochs=10, batch_size=128, validation_data=(x_test, x_test))

# Generate new images
n = 15
digit_size = 28
figure = np.zeros((digit_size * n, digit_size * n))

for i in range(n):
    for j in range(n):
        z_sample = np.array([[np.random.normal(), np.random.normal()]])
        x_decoded = decoder.predict(z_sample)
        digit = x_decoded[0].reshape(digit_size, digit_size)
        figure[i * digit_size: (i + 1) * digit_size, j * digit_size: (j + 1) * digit_size] = digit

plt.figure(figsize=(10, 10))
plt.imshow(figure, cmap='Greys_r')
plt.show()
```

This code defines a simple VAE architecture using TensorFlow and Keras, trains it on the MNIST dataset, and generates new images from the learned latent space. You can modify the architecture, dataset, and hyperparameters to suit your specific needs and applications.

Chapter 5 Generative Models for Text and Language

Recurrent Neural Networks (RNNs) for Sequence Generation

Recurrent Neural Networks (RNNs) are a class of neural networks particularly well-suited for sequence generation tasks, such as text generation, music composition, and speech synthesis. In this chapter, we'll explore how to use RNNs for sequence generation tasks, along with some practical applications and code examples:

1. **Introduction to Recurrent Neural Networks (RNNs)**:
    - Definition: RNNs are neural networks designed to process sequential data by maintaining an internal state or memory.

    - Time Series Data: RNNs are commonly used for processing time series data, where each input in the sequence depends on previous inputs.

    - Recurrent Connections: RNNs have recurrent connections that allow information to persist over time, making them suitable for modeling temporal dependencies.

Architecture of Recurrent Neural Networks:

- Recurrent Cells: The basic building block of RNNs is the recurrent cell, which takes an input and its previous state as input and produces an output and a new state.

- Long Short-Term Memory (LSTM) and Gated Recurrent Unit (GRU): Variants of RNNs, such as LSTMs and GRUs, are designed to address the vanishing gradient problem and capture long-term dependencies more effectively.

2. **Sequence Generation Tasks:**

    - Text Generation: RNNs can be trained to generate text character by character or word by word, allowing for the generation of realistic-sounding text passages, poetry, or dialogue.

    - Music Composition: RNNs trained on music sequences can generate new musical compositions, melodies, or harmonies, mimicking the style of the training data.

    - Speech Synthesis: RNNs can be used to generate speech waveforms or phoneme sequences, enabling the synthesis of human-like speech from text input.

3. **Training RNNs for Sequence Generation:**

    - Teacher Forcing: During training, RNNs are typically trained using a technique called teacher forcing, where the model is fed with the ground truth sequence at each time step.

    - Sampling: During inference or generation, RNNs generate output sequences by sampling from the probability distribution of the next token given the current input and hidden state.

4. **Practical Code Example:**

- We'll provide a Python code example using TensorFlow and Keras to train an RNN model for text generation. The model will be trained on a corpus of text data and used to generate new text sequences character by character.

By understanding how to use RNNs for sequence generation tasks and applying them in practical scenarios, practitioners can leverage the power of deep learning to generate realistic and creative sequences in various domains.

Basic Python code example demonstrating how to train a Recurrent Neural Network (RNN) for text generation using TensorFlow and Keras:

```python
import numpy as np
import tensorflow as tf
from tensorflow import keras
from tensorflow.keras import layers

# Load and preprocess text data
path_to_file = "path/to/your/text/file.txt"
text = open(path_to_file, "r").read()
vocab = sorted(set(text))
char2idx = {c: i for i, c in enumerate(vocab)}
idx2char = np.array(vocab)
text_as_int = np.array([char2idx[c] for c in text])

# Create training examples and targets
seq_length = 100
examples_per_epoch = len(text) // (seq_length + 1)
char_dataset = tf.data.Dataset.from_tensor_slices(text_as_int)
sequences = char_dataset.batch(seq_length + 1, drop_remainder=True)

def split_input_target(chunk):
    input_text = chunk[:-1]
    target_text = chunk[1:]
    return input_text, target_text

dataset = sequences.map(split_input_target)
BATCH_SIZE = 64
BUFFER_SIZE = 10000
dataset = dataset.shuffle(BUFFER_SIZE).batch(BATCH_SIZE, drop_remainder=True)
```

```python
# Define the RNN model
vocab_size = len(vocab)
embedding_dim = 256
rnn_units = 1024

def build_model(vocab_size, embedding_dim, rnn_units, batch_size):
    model = keras.Sequential([
        layers.Embedding(vocab_size, embedding_dim,
                batch_input_shape=[batch_size, None]),
        layers.LSTM(rnn_units,
                return_sequences=True,
                stateful=True,
                recurrent_initializer='glorot_uniform'),
        layers.Dense(vocab_size)
    ])
    return model

model = build_model(
    vocab_size=len(vocab),
    embedding_dim=embedding_dim,
    rnn_units=rnn_units,
    batch_size=BATCH_SIZE)

# Define loss function
def loss(labels, logits):
    return keras.losses.sparse_categorical_crossentropy(labels, logits, from_logits=True)

# Compile the model
model.compile(optimizer='adam', loss=loss)

# Train the model
history = model.fit(dataset, epochs=10)

# Generate text
def generate_text(model, start_string):
    num_generate = 1000
    input_eval = [char2idx[s] for s in start_string]
    input_eval = tf.expand_dims(input_eval, 0)
    text_generated = []
    temperature = 1.0

    model.reset_states()
```

```
for i in range(num_generate):
    predictions = model(input_eval)
    predictions = tf.squeeze(predictions, 0)
    predictions = predictions / temperature
    predicted_id = tf.random.categorical(predictions, num_samples=1)[-1,0].numpy()
    input_eval = tf.expand_dims([predicted_id], 0)
    text_generated.append(idx2char[predicted_id])

return (start_string + ''.join(text_generated))

print(generate_text(model, start_string=u"ROMEO: "))
```

This code trains an RNN model to generate text character by character. You can modify the **path_to_file** variable to point to your own text file. After training, the **generate_text** function can be used to generate new text sequences given a starting string. Adjust the parameters and model architecture as needed for your specific application.

Long Short-Term Memory Networks (LSTMs) and Gated Recurrent Units (GRUs)

Long Short-Term Memory (LSTM) networks and Gated Recurrent Units (GRUs) are popular variants of Recurrent Neural Networks (RNNs) designed to address the vanishing gradient problem and capture long-term dependencies more effectively. In this chapter, we'll explore LSTMs and GRUs in detail, discussing their architecture, advantages, and practical applications:

1. **Introduction to LSTMs and GRUs**:

    - **RNN Limitations**: Traditional RNNs struggle to capture long-term dependencies due to the vanishing gradient problem, where gradients diminish as they propagate through time steps.

- **Gated Mechanisms**: LSTMs and GRUs incorporate gated mechanisms that regulate the flow of information, allowing them to selectively retain or discard information over time.

2. **Architecture of LSTMs:**

    - **Forget Gate**: Determines which information to discard from the cell state.

    - **Input Gate**: Determines which new information to store in the cell state.

    - **Output Gate**: Determines which information to output from the cell state.

    - **Cell State**: Internal memory that runs along the entire sequence, allowing LSTMs to maintain information over long periods.

3. **Architecture of GRUs:**

    - **Update Gate**: Controls the flow of Information, determining how much of the past information to keep and how much of the new information to add.

    - **Reset Gate**: Determines how much of the past information to forget.

4. **Advantages of LSTMs and GRUs:**

    - **Capturing Long-Term Dependencies**: LSTMs and GRUs excel at capturing long-range dependencies in sequential data, making them suitable for tasks involving context understanding and memory retention.

    - **Reducing Vanishing Gradient Problem**: The gated mechanisms in LSTMs and GRUs help alleviate the vanishing gradient problem, enabling more effective training of deep recurrent networks.

5. **Applications of LSTMs and GRUs**:

    - **Natural Language Processing**: LSTMs and GRUs are widely used for tasks such as language modeling, machine translation, sentiment analysis, and named entity recognition.

    - **Time Series Prediction**: LSTMs and GRUs are effective for modeling and predicting time series data in domains such as finance, weather forecasting, and stock market analysis.

    - **Speech Recognition**: LSTMs and GRUs are employed in speech recognition systems to transcribe spoken language into text.

6. **Practical Code Examples**:

    - We'll provide Python code examples using TensorFlow and Keras to implement LSTMs and GRUs for sequence prediction tasks, such as time series forecasting or text generation.

By understanding the architecture and advantages of LSTMs and GRUs, practitioners can effectively leverage these advanced recurrent architectures for a wide range of sequential data analysis tasks.

Transformers and Attention Mechanisms

Transformers and attention mechanisms represent a breakthrough in natural language processing (NLP) and sequential data processing. In this chapter, we'll delve into the fundamentals of Transformers and attention mechanisms, their architecture, and their applications:

1. **Introduction to Transformers**:

    - **Motivation**: Traditional sequential models, such as RNNs and LSTMs, have limitations in capturing long-range dependencies efficiently. Transformers were introduced as a novel architecture to address these limitations.

    - **Key Features**: Transformers rely on self-attention mechanisms to weigh the importance of different input elements, enabling parallel computation and capturing long-range dependencies effectively.

2. **Architecture of Transformers**:

    - **Self-Attention Mechanism**: Each input element is associated with an attention score computed based on its relationship with other elements in the sequence.

    - **Transformer Blocks**: Transformers consist of multiple layers of self-attention mechanisms and feed-forward neural networks.

    - **Positional Encoding**: Since Transformers do not inherently understand the order of input sequences, positional encoding is added to provide positional information to the model.

    - **Encoder-Decoder Architecture:** Transformers can be used for both encoder and decoder tasks in sequence-to-sequence learning tasks.

3. **Attention Mechanisms**:

    - **Scaled Dot-Product Attention**: The core attention mechanism in Transformers, where each input element is associated with a weight computed based on its relevance to other elements.

- **Multi-Head Attention**: Transformers use multiple attention heads to capture different aspects of the input sequence simultaneously, enabling richer representations.

- **Self-Attention vs. Global Attention**: Self-attention mechanisms focus on relationships within the input sequence, while global attention mechanisms consider relationships with external context.

4. **Advantages of Transformers**:

    - **Efficient Parallelization**: Transformers enable efficient parallelization of computation due to their attention-based architecture, leading to faster training and inference.

    - **Capturing Long-Range Dependencies**: Transformers excel at capturing long-range dependencies in sequential data, making them suitable for tasks requiring context understanding and global reasoning.

5. **Applications of Transformers**:

    - **Natural Language Processing**: Transformers have revolutionized NLP tasks such as language modeling, machine translation, text summarization, and question answering.

    - **Image Processing**: Transformers have been adapted for image processing tasks such as image classification, object detection, and image generation.

6. **Practical Code Examples**:

    - We'll provide Python code examples using popular deep learning libraries such as TensorFlow and

PyTorch to implement Transformers for various NLP tasks, such as text classification or language translation.

By understanding the architecture and capabilities of Transformers and attention mechanisms, practitioners can leverage these powerful models to tackle a wide range of sequential data processing tasks more effectively than traditional sequential models.

Text Generation with GPT (Generative Pre-trained Transformer) Models

Text Generation with Generative Pre-trained Transformer (GPT) models represents one of the most advanced and widely-used applications of Transformer-based architectures. In this chapter, we'll explore the principles of text generation using GPT models, their architecture, and practical applications:

1. **Introduction to GPT Models**:

    - **Background**: GPT models are a family of autoregressive language models developed by OpenAI, based on the Transformer architecture.

    - **Pre-training**: GPT models are pre-trained on large corpora of text data using unsupervised learning objectives, such as masked language modeling or next sentence prediction.

    - **Fine-tuning**: After pre-training, GPT models can be fine-tuned on specific downstream tasks, such as text generation, text classification, or language understanding.

2. **Architecture of GPT Models**:

- **Transformer-Based**: GPT models are based on the Transformer architecture, consisting of multiple layers of self-attention mechanisms and feed-forward neural networks.

- **Unidirectional Context**: GPT models generate text in a left-to-right manner, conditioning each token on the preceding context.

- **Positional Embeddings**: GPT models use positional embeddings to provide positional information to the model, allowing it to understand the order of tokens in the input sequence.

3. **Text Generation with GPT Models**:

    - **Autoregressive Generation**: GPT models generate text autoregressively, predicting each token based on the preceding context.

    - **Sampling Strategies**: Various sampling strategies can be used to generate text with GPT models, including greedy decoding, beam search, nucleus sampling, and top-k sampling.

    - **Controlled Generation**: GPT models can be conditioned on specific prompts or attributes to generate text with desired characteristics or styles.

4. **Applications of GPT Models**:

    - **Content Creation**: GPT models are used for content generation tasks such as story generation, dialogue generation, poetry generation, and creative writing.

    - **Chatbots and Virtual Assistants**: GPT-based chatbots and virtual assistants can engage in human-like conversations, answering questions and providing information.

- **Code Generation**: GPT models can generate code snippets and programming scripts based on high-level descriptions or natural language prompts.

5. **Ethical Considerations and Challenges**:

    - **Bias and Fairness**: GPT models trained on large corpora of text data may inadvertently perpetuate biases present in the training data.

    - **Misinformation and Manipulation**: GPT models can be used to generate fake news, propaganda, or misleading content, raising concerns about misinformation and manipulation.

6. **Practical Code Examples**:

    - We'll provide Python code examples using Hugging Face's Transformers library to fine-tune and generate text with pre-trained GPT models such as GPT-2 or GPT-3.

By understanding the principles and applications of text generation with GPT models, practitioners can harness the power of state-of-the-art natural language processing technology for various creative, informational, and conversational tasks.

Basic Python code example demonstrating how to generate text using a pre-trained GPT model from the Hugging Face Transformers library:

```
from transformers import GPT2LMHeadModel, GPT2Tokenizer

# Load pre-trained GPT model and tokenizer
model_name = "gpt2-medium"  # You can choose from various model sizes such as "gpt2", "gpt2-medium", "gpt2-large", "gpt2-xl"
tokenizer = GPT2Tokenizer.from_pretrained(model_name)
model = GPT2LMHeadModel.from_pretrained(model_name)

# Set seed for reproducibility
```

```python
import torch
torch.manual_seed(42)

# Define input text
input_text = "Once upon a time,"

# Tokenize input text
input_ids = tokenizer.encode(input_text, return_tensors="pt")

# Generate text
max_length = 100  # Maximum length of generated text
output = model.generate(input_ids, max_length=max_length,
num_return_sequences=1,                temperature=0.7,
pad_token_id=tokenizer.eos_token_id)

# Decode and print generated text
generated_text         =        tokenizer.decode(output[0],
skip_special_tokens=True)
print(generated_text)
```

In this code:

- We first import the necessary modules from the Transformers library, including the GPT2LMHeadModel and GPT2Tokenizer.

- We specify the name of the pre-trained GPT model we want to use (e.g., "gpt2-medium").

- We load the pre-trained GPT model and tokenizer using the specified model name.

- We set a random seed for reproducibility.

- We define an input text that serves as a prompt for text generation.

- We tokenize the input text using the tokenizer.

- We use the model's generate method to generate text based on the input_ids, specifying the maximum length of the generated text, the number of sequences to generate, the temperature (a hyperparameter controlling the randomness of the generated text), and the pad_token_id (the token ID used for padding).

Finally, we decode the generated text and print it.
You can adjust the input_text and other parameters according to your specific application and requirements. Additionally, you can fine-tune the model on your own dataset for better performance on specific text generation tasks.

Chapter 6 Image Generation with GANs

StyleGAN and StyleGAN2: High-Quality Image Synthesis

StyleGAN and StyleGAN2 are state-of-the-art generative adversarial network (GAN) architectures designed for high-quality image synthesis. In this chapter, we'll explore the principles behind StyleGAN and StyleGAN2, their architecture, and applications in generating realistic images:

1. **Introduction to StyleGAN and StyleGAN2**:

    - **Motivation**: Traditional GAN models often produce low-resolution or low-quality images with artifacts. StyleGAN and StyleGAN2 were developed to address these limitations and generate high-quality, diverse, and realistic images.

2. **Architecture of StyleGAN**:

    - **Mapping Network**: Converts latent vectors sampled from a standard normal distribution into intermediate latent vectors.

    - **Style Mixing Regularization**: Encourages disentanglement of different aspects of variation, allowing for more fine-grained control over generated images.

- **Progressive Growing**: Gradually increases the resolution of generated images during training, starting from low resolution and incrementally adding layers for higher resolution.

3. **Architecture of StyleGAN2**:

    - **Improved Generator Architecture**: StyleGAN2 introduces several architectural improvements over StyleGAN, including a more efficient generator network design and enhanced regularization techniques.

    - **Path Length Regularization**: Encourages smooth and diverse latent space traversals, leading to more stable training and improved image quality.

    - **Adaptive Discriminator Augmentation**: Dynamically adjusts data augmentation techniques applied to discriminator inputs during training, improving robustness and generalization.

4. **Advantages of StyleGAN and StyleGAN2**:

    - **High-Quality Image Synthesis**: StyleGAN and StyleGAN2 produce high-resolution, photorealistic images with fine details and rich textures.

    - **Fine-Grained Control**: These models allow for fine-grained control over various aspects of generated images, such as facial attributes, pose, and style.

    - **Diverse Image Generation**: StyleGAN and StyleGAN2 can generate diverse and novel images across different domains, from human faces to artwork and landscapes.

5. **Applications of StyleGAN and StyleGAN2**:

- **Art Generation**: These models are used to generate digital art, portraits, and creative designs.

- **Face Generation**: StyleGAN and StyleGAN2 are commonly used in face generation applications, including generating photorealistic human faces for avatars, gaming, and virtual reality.

- **Data Augmentation**: These models can augment datasets for various computer vision tasks, such as object detection and image classification.

6. **Challenges and Limitations**:

   - **Complexity and Resource Requirements**: Training StyleGAN and StyleGAN2 requires significant computational resources and expertise.

   - **Mode Collapse**: Like other GAN models, StyleGAN and StyleGAN2 are prone to mode collapse, where the generator produces limited diversity in generated images.

7. **Future Directions**:

   - **Improving Training Stability**: Research continues to focus on improving the stability and robustness of training GAN models.

   - **Exploring New Applications**: StyleGAN and StyleGAN2 open up possibilities for new applications in areas such as fashion, interior design, and visual effects.

By understanding the architecture and capabilities of StyleGAN and StyleGAN2, practitioners can leverage these advanced generative models for various image synthesis tasks, from artistic creation to data augmentation and beyond.

A simplified example using TensorFlow and the official StyleGAN2 implementation from NVlabs:

Implementing StyleGAN and StyleGAN2 from scratch in Python is a complex task due to their intricate architectures and large-scale training requirements. However, you can utilize pre-trained models and libraries such as TensorFlow or PyTorch to generate images using these architectures. Here's a simplified example using TensorFlow and the official StyleGAN2 implementation

```
from NVlabs
import numpy as np
import tensorflow as tf
import dnnlib.tflib as tflib
import pretrained_networks

# Load pre-trained StyleGAN2 model
network_pkl = 'gdrive:networks/stylegan2-ffhq-config-f.pkl'   # Example path to pre-trained StyleGAN2 model
_G, _D, Gs = pretrained_networks.load_networks(network_pkl)

# Generate random latent vector
latent_size = Gs.input_shape[1]
latent_vector = np.random.randn(1, latent_size)

# Generate image from latent vector
with tf.Session() as sess:
    sess.run(tf.global_variables_initializer())
    images = Gs.run(latent_vector, None, truncation_psi=0.7, randomize_noise=True,
    output_transform=dict(func=tflib.convert_images_to_uint8))

# Display generated image
import matplotlib.pyplot as plt
plt.imshow(images[0])
plt.axis('off')
plt.show()
```

In this code:

- We import necessary libraries including TensorFlow, StyleGAN2 implementation from NVlabs, and matplotlib for image visualization.

- We load a pre-trained StyleGAN2 model using **pretrained_networks.load_networks()** function from the official StyleGAN2 implementation.

- We generate a random latent vector of the appropriate size for the StyleGAN2 model.

- We use the pre-trained StyleGAN2 model to generate an image from the random latent vector.

- Finally, we display the generated image using matplotlib.

Before running this code, you need to install the required dependencies and download the pre-trained StyleGAN2 model. Additionally, ensure that you have the necessary resources, including a compatible GPU, for running StyleGAN2 inference.

Conditional Image Generation

Conditional image generation refers to the process of generating images based on specific conditions or attributes provided as input to the generative model. This allows for controlling and guiding the generation process to produce images with desired characteristics. In this chapter, we'll explore the principles of conditional image generation and how it can be implemented using deep learning models, particularly conditional generative adversarial networks (cGANs) and conditional variational autoencoders (cVAEs):

1. **Introduction to Conditional Image Generation**:

    - **Motivation**: Traditional generative models such as GANs and VAEs generate images without explicit control over their attributes. Conditional image generation enables specifying desired attributes or conditions to guide the generation process.

    - **Applications**: Conditional image generation has applications in various domains, including image-to-image translation, style transfer, image editing, and content creation.

2. **Conditional Generative Adversarial Networks (cGANs):**

    - **Architecture:** cGANs extend the standard GAN architecture by conditioning both the generator and discriminator networks on additional input information, such as class labels or attribute vectors.

    - **Training:** During training, both the generator and discriminator are conditioned on the desired attributes, enabling the generation of images with specific characteristics.

    - **Applications:** cGANs are used for tasks such as conditional image synthesis, image-to-image translation (e.g., translating sketches to photos, day to night conversion), and attribute manipulation (e.g., changing hair color, age progression).

3. **Conditional Variational Autoencoders (cVAEs):**

    - **Architecture:** cVAEs combine the encoder-decoder architecture of VAEs with conditioning mechanisms to generate images conditioned on specific attributes or conditions.

    - **Latent Space Manipulation:** By controlling the attributes in the latent space, cVAEs allow for the generation of images with desired attributes or styles.

    - **Applications:** cVAEs are used for tasks such as image generation with specific attributes, style transfer, and image editing (e.g., adding or removing objects, changing backgrounds).

4. **Training Strategies and Techniques:**

- **Attribute Embedding**: Encoding attributes into a low-dimensional embedding space to provide as input to the generator or decoder network.

- **Conditional Loss Functions**: Designing loss functions that encourage the generator to produce images consistent with the specified attributes.

- **Data Augmentation**: Augmenting training data with attribute labels or conditions to improve model generalization.

5. **Practical Code Examples**:

   - We'll provide Python code examples using popular deep learning frameworks such as TensorFlow or PyTorch to implement conditional image generation with cGANs and cVAEs.

By understanding the principles and techniques of conditional image generation, practitioners can develop sophisticated generative models capable of producing images with specific attributes, styles, and characteristics, opening up new possibilities for creative applications and content generation.

Implementing conditional image generation in Python

Implementing conditional image generation in Python involves using deep learning frameworks such as TensorFlow or PyTorch to build conditional generative models like conditional generative adversarial networks (cGANs) or conditional variational autoencoders (cVAEs). Below is a simplified example of conditional image generation using a cGAN with TensorFlow:Top of Form

```
import numpy as np
import matplotlib.pyplot as plt
import tensorflow as tf
```

```python
from tensorflow.keras.layers import Dense, Reshape, Flatten, Conv2D, Conv2DTranspose
from tensorflow.keras.models import Sequential

# Generate synthetic data
def generate_data(n_samples=1000):
    x = np.random.uniform(-1, 1, size=(n_samples, 100))  # Latent vectors
    labels = np.random.randint(0, 10, size=n_samples)  # Random labels (classes)
    images = np.zeros((n_samples, 28, 28, 1))  # Placeholder for images
    for i in range(n_samples):
        images[i] = generate_image(x[i], labels[i])
    return x, labels, images

# Generate image from latent vector and label
def generate_image(latent_vector, label):
    model = Sequential([
        Dense(7*7*128, input_dim=100),
        Reshape((7, 7, 128)),
        Conv2DTranspose(128, (4, 4), strides=(2, 2), padding='same', activation='relu'),
        Conv2DTranspose(64, (4, 4), strides=(2, 2), padding='same', activation='relu'),
        Conv2DTranspose(1, (4, 4), strides=(1, 1), padding='same', activation='sigmoid')
    ])
    noise = np.random.normal(0, 0.2, size=(1, 100))  # Add noise to the latent vector
    generated_image = model.predict(latent_vector + noise)
    return generated_image

# Define the discriminator model
def discriminator_model():
    model = Sequential([
        Conv2D(64, (3, 3), strides=(2, 2), padding='same', input_shape=(28, 28, 1)),
        Conv2D(128, (3, 3), strides=(2, 2), padding='same'),
        Flatten(),
        Dense(1, activation='sigmoid')
    ])
    return model

# Define the generator model
```

```python
def generator_model():
    model = Sequential([
        Dense(7*7*128, input_dim=110),
        Reshape((7, 7, 128)),
        Conv2DTranspose(128, (4, 4), strides=(2, 2), padding='same', activation='relu'),
        Conv2DTranspose(64, (4, 4), strides=(2, 2), padding='same', activation='relu'),
        Conv2DTranspose(1, (4, 4), strides=(1, 1), padding='same', activation='sigmoid')
    ])
    return model

# Define the conditional GAN model
def cgan_model(generator, discriminator):
    discriminator.trainable = False
    model = Sequential([generator, discriminator])
    return model

# Train the conditional GAN model
def train_cgan(generator, discriminator, cgan, x, labels, epochs=100, batch_size=128):
    cgan.compile(loss='binary_crossentropy', optimizer='adam')
    for epoch in range(epochs):
        idx = np.random.randint(0, x.shape[0], batch_size)
        real_images = x[idx]
        real_labels = labels[idx]
        real_labels = tf.keras.utils.to_categorical(real_labels, 10)
        fake_labels = np.random.randint(0, 10, size=batch_size)
        fake_labels = tf.keras.utils.to_categorical(fake_labels, 10)
        fake_images = generator.predict([np.random.normal(0, 1, size=(batch_size, 100)), fake_labels])
        real_loss = discriminator.train_on_batch(real_images, real_labels)
        fake_loss = discriminator.train_on_batch(fake_images, fake_labels)
        combined_loss = cgan.train_on_batch([np.random.normal(0, 1, size=(batch_size, 100)), fake_labels], real_labels)
        print(f'Epoch: {epoch + 1}, Real Loss: {real_loss}, Fake Loss: {fake_loss}, Combined Loss: {combined_loss}')

# Generate conditional images
def generate_conditional_images(generator, labels):
    n_samples = len(labels)
```

```
    latent_vectors = np.random.normal(0, 1, size=(n_samples,
100))
    labels = tf.keras.utils.to_categorical(labels, 10)
    generated_images = generator.predict([latent_vectors,
labels])
    return generated_images

# Generate synthetic data
x, labels, images = generate_data()

# Build discriminator and generator models
discriminator = discriminator_model()
generator = generator_model()

# Build conditional GAN model
cgan = cgan_model(generator, discriminator)

# Train conditional GAN
train_cgan(generator, discriminator, cgan, x, labels)

# Generate conditional images
conditional_labels = np.random.randint(0, 10, size=10)    #
Random conditional labels
generated_images = generate_conditional_images(generator,
conditional_labels)

# Display generated images
plt.figure(figsize=(10, 1))
for i in range(10):
    plt.subplot(1, 10, i+1)
    plt.imshow(generated_images[i].reshape(28,          28),
cmap='gray')
    plt.axis('off')
plt.show()
```

In this code:

- We first generate synthetic data consisting of latent vectors and corresponding labels.
- We define functions to build the discriminator and generator models.
- We define the conditional GAN model by combining the generator and discriminator.
- We train the conditional GAN model using the synthetic data.

- Finally, we generate conditional images by providing random conditional labels to the generator.

Note: This code is a simplified example for demonstration purposes and may require modifications for specific use cases and datasets. Additionally, ensure that you have the necessary dependencies installed, including TensorFlow and Matplotlib.

Image-to-Image Translation: Pix2Pix, CycleGAN, etc.

Image-to-image translation refers to the task of converting an image from one domain to another while preserving the semantic content of the input image. This process is typically achieved using deep learning models trained on paired or unpaired data. In this section, we'll explore popular image-to-image translation techniques such as Pix2Pix and CycleGAN:

1. **Introduction to Image-to-Image Translation**:

    - **Definition**: Image-to-image translation aims to transform images from one domain to another, such as converting satellite images to maps, day scenes to night scenes, or sketches to photos.

    - **Applications**: Image-to-image translation has applications in various domains, including computer vision, graphics, medical imaging, and augmented reality.

2. **Pix2Pix**:

    - **Architecture**: Pix2Pix is a conditional generative adversarial network (cGAN) architecture that learns a mapping from input images to output images in a supervised manner.

- **Training**: Pix2Pix requires paired training data, where each input image is paired with a corresponding target output image.

- **Loss Functions**: Pix2Pix uses adversarial loss, L1 loss, and optionally other losses such as feature matching loss to train the generator and discriminator networks.

- **Applications**: Pix2Pix has been applied to tasks such as image colorization, semantic segmentation, and image super-resolution.

3. **CycleGAN**:

    - **Architecture**: CycleGAN is an unsupervised image-to-image translation model that learns mappings between two image domains without paired training data.

    - **Cycle-Consistency Loss**: CycleGAN introduces a cycle-consistency loss, which enforces that the translation from domain A to domain B and back to domain A should recover the original input image.

    - **Applications**: CycleGAN has been used for style transfer, artistic image synthesis, domain adaptation, and domain transfer tasks.

4. **Applications and Extensions**:

    - **Extensions**: Variants and extensions of Pix2Pix and CycleGAN, such as BicycleGAN, DualGAN, and DiscoGAN, introduce additional constraints or modifications to improve performance or handle specific tasks.

    - **Real-World Applications**: Image-to-image translation techniques have practical applications in fields such as urban planning, image editing software, fashion design, and medical imaging.

5. **Practical Implementation**:

    - We'll provide Python code examples using popular deep learning frameworks such as TensorFlow or PyTorch to implement Pix2Pix and CycleGAN for image-to-image translation tasks.

By understanding the principles and techniques of image-to-image translation, practitioners can develop models capable of transforming images between different domains, opening up new possibilities for creative applications, data augmentation, and domain adaptation in various domains.

Implementing Pix2Pix for image-to-image translation in Python

Implementing Pix2Pix for image-to-image translation in Python involves building a conditional generative adversarial network (cGAN) architecture and training it using paired image data. Below is a simplified example of Pix2Pix implementation using TensorFlow:

```
import tensorflow as tf
from tensorflow.keras.layers import Input, Concatenate, Conv2D, Conv2DTranspose
from tensorflow.keras.models import Model
from tensorflow.keras.losses import BinaryCrossentropy, MeanAbsoluteError
from tensorflow.keras.optimizers import Adam
from tensorflow.keras.callbacks import ModelCheckpoint
import numpy as np

# Define the generator model
def build_generator(input_shape=(256, 256, 3)):
    # Encoder
    inputs = Input(shape=input_shape)
    conv1 = Conv2D(64, (4, 4), strides=(2, 2), padding='same', activation='relu')(inputs)
```

```python
    conv2 = Conv2D(128, (4, 4), strides=(2, 2), padding='same',
activation='relu')(conv1)
    conv3 = Conv2D(256, (4, 4), strides=(2, 2), padding='same',
activation='relu')(conv2)
    conv4 = Conv2D(512, (4, 4), strides=(2, 2), padding='same',
activation='relu')(conv3)
    conv5 = Conv2D(512, (4, 4), strides=(2, 2), padding='same',
activation='relu')(conv4)
    conv6 = Conv2D(512, (4, 4), strides=(2, 2), padding='same',
activation='relu')(conv5)
    conv7 = Conv2D(512, (4, 4), strides=(2, 2), padding='same',
activation='relu')(conv6)
    conv8 = Conv2D(512, (4, 4), strides=(2, 2), padding='same',
activation='relu')(conv7)

    # Decoder
    deconv1 = Conv2DTranspose(512, (4, 4), strides=(2, 2),
padding='same', activation='relu')(conv8)
    merge1 = Concatenate()([deconv1, conv7])
    deconv2 = Conv2DTranspose(512, (4, 4), strides=(2, 2),
padding='same', activation='relu')(merge1)
    merge2 = Concatenate()([deconv2, conv6])
    deconv3 = Conv2DTranspose(512, (4, 4), strides=(2, 2),
padding='same', activation='relu')(merge2)
    merge3 = Concatenate()([deconv3, conv5])
    deconv4 = Conv2DTranspose(512, (4, 4), strides=(2, 2),
padding='same', activation='relu')(merge3)
    merge4 = Concatenate()([deconv4, conv4])
    deconv5 = Conv2DTranspose(256, (4, 4), strides=(2, 2),
padding='same', activation='relu')(merge4)
    merge5 = Concatenate()([deconv5, conv3])
    deconv6 = Conv2DTranspose(128, (4, 4), strides=(2, 2),
padding='same', activation='relu')(merge5)
    merge6 = Concatenate()([deconv6, conv2])
    deconv7 = Conv2DTranspose(64, (4, 4), strides=(2, 2),
padding='same', activation='relu')(merge6)
    merge7 = Concatenate()([deconv7, conv1])
    deconv8 = Conv2DTranspose(3, (4, 4), strides=(2, 2),
padding='same', activation='tanh')(merge7)

    model = Model(inputs=inputs, outputs=deconv8)
    return model

# Define the discriminator model
def build_discriminator(input_shape=(256, 256, 6)):
```

```python
    inputs = Input(shape=input_shape)
    conv1 = Conv2D(64, (4, 4), strides=(2, 2), padding='same', activation='relu')(inputs)
    conv2 = Conv2D(128, (4, 4), strides=(2, 2), padding='same', activation='relu')(conv1)
    conv3 = Conv2D(256, (4, 4), strides=(2, 2), padding='same', activation='relu')(conv2)
    conv4 = Conv2D(512, (4, 4), strides=(2, 2), padding='same', activation='relu')(conv3)
    outputs = Conv2D(1, (4, 4), strides=(2, 2), padding='same', activation='sigmoid')(conv4)
    model = Model(inputs=inputs, outputs=outputs)
    return model

# Define the combined model (Pix2Pix)
def build_pix2pix(generator, discriminator, input_shape=(256, 256, 3)):
    generator_input = Input(shape=input_shape)
    discriminator_input = Input(shape=(input_shape[0], input_shape[1], input_shape[2] * 2))
    generated_images = generator(generator_input)
    outputs = discriminator(Concatenate()([generator_input, generated_images]))
    model = Model(inputs=[generator_input, discriminator_input], outputs=outputs)
    return model

# Define loss functions
binary_crossentropy_loss = BinaryCrossentropy()
mean_absolute_error_loss = MeanAbsoluteError()

# Build and compile the models
generator = build_generator()
discriminator = build_discriminator()
pix2pix_model = build_pix2pix(generator, discriminator)
pix2pix_model.compile(optimizer=Adam(learning_rate=0.0002, beta_1=0.5), loss=binary_crossentropy_loss)

# Train the model (Example: Training loop)

# Assuming X_train contains paired input images and target output images
# where X_train[0] is the input image and X_train[1] is the target output image
```

```
for epoch in range(num_epochs):
    for batch in range(num_batches):
        batch_indices = np.random.randint(0, len(X_train), batch_size)
        batch_images = X_train[batch_indices]
        generated_images = generator.predict(batch_images[0]) # Generate images using the generator
        fake_input = np.concatenate([batch_images[0], generated_images], axis=-1)
        real_input = np.concatenate([batch_images[0], batch_images[1]], axis=-1)
        discriminator_input = np.concatenate([real_input, fake_input], axis=0)
        discriminator_labels = np.concatenate([np.ones((batch_size, 1)), np.zeros((batch_size, 1))], axis=0)
        discriminator_loss = pix2pix_model.train_on_batch([batch_images[0], discriminator_input], discriminator_labels)
        generator_loss = pix2pix_model.train_on_batch([batch_images[0], discriminator_input], np.ones((batch_size, 1)))
```

This code provides a basic implementation of Pix2Pix for image-to-image translation using TensorFlow. However, for practical use cases, additional modifications, optimizations, and considerations (such as data preprocessing, data augmentation, and model tuning) may be necessary.

Super-Resolution and Image Inpainting with GANs

Super-resolution and image inpainting with Generative Adversarial Networks (GANs) are advanced techniques in computer vision that aim to enhance the quality of images or fill in missing parts of images. Below is an outline of these topics along with their applications and potential Python code implementations:

1. **Introduction to Super-Resolution:**

    - **Definition:** Super-resolution refers to the process of increasing the resolution or enhancing the quality of low-resolution images to generate high-resolution versions.

    - **Applications:** Super-resolution techniques are commonly used in medical imaging, satellite imaging, surveillance systems, and enhancing digital photographs.

2. **Generative Adversarial Networks (GANs):**

    - **Overview:** GANs are a type of deep learning model consisting of two neural networks, a generator and a discriminator, trained adversarially to generate realistic data.

    - **Training:** GANs are trained using a minimax game where the generator tries to produce realistic images to fool the discriminator, while the discriminator learns to distinguish between real and fake images.

3. **Super-Resolution with GANs:**

    - **Architecture:** Super-resolution GANs (SRGANs) utilize GAN architecture to generate high-resolution images from low-resolution inputs.

    - **Loss Functions:** SRGANs typically use perceptual loss functions, such as content loss and adversarial loss, to train the generator network.

    - **Applications:** SRGANs can be applied to enhance the resolution of images captured by low-resolution cameras or to upscale low-quality video frames.

4. **Image Inpainting with GANs:**

- **Definition**: Image inpainting refers to the process of filling in missing or damaged parts of images to reconstruct the original scene.

- **Techniques**: GAN-based inpainting methods generate plausible content to complete missing regions based on the surrounding context.

- **Applications**: Image inpainting has applications in photo editing, image restoration, and removing unwanted objects from images.

5. **Python Code Implementation**:

    - **Libraries**: Implementations of super-resolution and image inpainting with GANs can be found in deep learning frameworks such as TensorFlow or PyTorch.

    - **Example Code**: Python code examples demonstrating super-resolution and image inpainting with GANs can be provided to illustrate the implementation process.

By understanding super-resolution and image inpainting techniques using GANs, practitioners can develop models capable of enhancing image quality and reconstructing missing parts of images, which have various applications in digital image processing and computer vision tasks.

A simplified Python code example for implementing super-resolution and image inpainting using Generative Adversarial Networks (GANs) with TensorFlow:

```
import tensorflow as tf
from tensorflow.keras.layers import Input, Conv2D, Conv2DTranspose
from tensorflow.keras.models import Model
from tensorflow.keras.losses import BinaryCrossentropy, MeanAbsoluteError
from tensorflow.keras.optimizers import Adam
import numpy as np
```

```python
# Define the generator model for super-resolution
def build_super_resolution_generator(input_shape=(64, 64, 3), scale_factor=4):
    inputs = Input(shape=input_shape)
    # Encoder
    conv1 = Conv2D(64, (3, 3), padding='same', activation='relu')(inputs)
    # Decoder
    deconv1 = Conv2DTranspose(64, (3, 3), strides=(scale_factor, scale_factor), padding='same', activation='relu')(conv1)
    outputs = Conv2D(3, (3, 3), padding='same', activation='sigmoid')(deconv1)
    model = Model(inputs=inputs, outputs=outputs)
    return model

# Define the generator model for image inpainting
def build_image_inpainting_generator(input_shape=(64, 64, 3)):
    inputs = Input(shape=input_shape)
    # Encoder
    conv1 = Conv2D(64, (3, 3), padding='same', activation='relu')(inputs)
    # Decoder
    deconv1 = Conv2DTranspose(64, (3, 3), padding='same', activation='relu')(conv1)
    outputs = Conv2D(3, (3, 3), padding='same', activation='sigmoid')(deconv1)
    model = Model(inputs=inputs, outputs=outputs)
    return model

# Define loss functions
binary_crossentropy_loss = BinaryCrossentropy()
mean_absolute_error_loss = MeanAbsoluteError()

# Build and compile the super-resolution generator model
super_resolution_generator = build_super_resolution_generator()
super_resolution_generator.compile(optimizer=Adam(learning_rate=0.0002), loss=mean_absolute_error_loss)

# Build and compile the image inpainting generator model
image_inpainting_generator = build_image_inpainting_generator()
```

```
image_inpainting_generator.compile(optimizer=Adam(learning_rate=0.0002), loss=mean_absolute_error_loss)

# Training loop for super-resolution (Example)
for epoch in range(num_epochs):
    for batch in range(num_batches):
        # Load batch of low-resolution images and corresponding high-resolution images
        batch_lr_images, batch_hr_images = load_batch()
        # Train the super-resolution generator
        super_resolution_loss = super_resolution_generator.train_on_batch(batch_lr_images, batch_hr_images)

# Training loop for image inpainting (Example)
for epoch in range(num_epochs):
    for batch in range(num_batches):
        # Load batch of incomplete images and corresponding ground truth images
        batch_incomplete_images, batch_complete_images = load_batch()
        # Train the image inpainting generator
        inpainting_loss = image_inpainting_generator.train_on_batch(batch_incomplete_images, batch_complete_images)
```

This code provides a basic implementation of super-resolution and image inpainting using GANs with TensorFlow. Actual implementations may require additional components such as discriminator networks, adversarial training, and more sophisticated architectures. Additionally, data loading, preprocessing, and evaluation steps need to be incorporated for practical usage.

Chapter 7 Generative Models for Music and Audio

Music generation with Long Short-Term Memory (LSTM) networks and Variational Autoencoders (VAEs) is an exciting application of deep learning in the field of music composition. Below is an outline of this topic along with its potential applications and Python code implementations:

1. **Introduction to Music Generation**:

    - **Definition**: Music generation involves using machine learning algorithms to create new musical compositions autonomously.

    - **Applications**: Music generation has applications in various fields such as entertainment, education, and creative arts.

    - **Example**: Here's a simplified Python code example for generating music using a Generative Adversarial Network (GAN) with TensorFlow:

```
import numpy as np
import tensorflow as tf
from tensorflow.keras.layers import Dense, Reshape, BatchNormalization, LeakyReLU, Input
from tensorflow.keras.models import Sequential, Model
```

```python
from tensorflow.keras.optimizers import Adam

# Define the generator model
def build_generator(latent_dim, output_shape):
    model = Sequential([
        Dense(256, input_dim=latent_dim),
        LeakyReLU(alpha=0.2),
        BatchNormalization(),
        Dense(512),
        LeakyReLU(alpha=0.2),
        BatchNormalization(),
        Dense(1024),
        LeakyReLU(alpha=0.2),
        BatchNormalization(),
        Dense(np.prod(output_shape), activation='tanh'),
        Reshape(output_shape)
    ])
    return model

# Define the discriminator model
def build_discriminator(input_shape):
    model = Sequential([
        Flatten(input_shape=input_shape),
        Dense(512),
        LeakyReLU(alpha=0.2),
        Dense(256),
        LeakyReLU(alpha=0.2),
        Dense(1, activation='sigmoid')
    ])
    return model

# Define the GAN model
def build_gan(generator, discriminator):
    discriminator.trainable = False
    gan_input = Input(shape=(latent_dim,))
    generated_music = generator(gan_input)
    gan_output = discriminator(generated_music)
    gan = Model(gan_input, gan_output)
    gan.compile(loss='binary_crossentropy', optimizer=Adam(lr=0.0002, beta_1=0.5))
    return gan

# Define the parameters
latent_dim = 100
```

```
output_shape = (num_timesteps, num_features)    # Adjust
according to your music data format
num_epochs = 1000
batch_size = 128

# Build and compile the generator and discriminator
generator = build_generator(latent_dim, output_shape)
discriminator = build_discriminator(output_shape)
gan = build_gan(generator, discriminator)

# Train the GAN
for epoch in range(num_epochs):
    for _ in range(num_batches):
        # Sample random noise for generator input
        noise = np.random.normal(0, 1, (batch_size, latent_dim))
        # Generate music samples
        generated_music = generator.predict(noise)
        # Get real music samples
        real_music = get_real_music_batch()   # Implement your own function to get real music data
        # Train discriminator
        d_loss_real = discriminator.train_on_batch(real_music, np.ones((batch_size, 1)))
        d_loss_fake = discriminator.train_on_batch(generated_music, np.zeros((batch_size, 1)))
        # Train generator
        noise = np.random.normal(0, 1, (batch_size, latent_dim))
        g_loss = gan.train_on_batch(noise, np.ones((batch_size, 1)))
```

This code sets up a simple GAN architecture for music generation using TensorFlow. You'll need to replace **get_real_music_batch()** with your own function to fetch real music data in batches. Additionally, make sure to adjust the **output_shape** according to the format of your music data. Further optimizations and adjustments may be needed based on your specific requirements and dataset characteristics.

2. **Music Generation with LSTM Networks**:

   - **Architecture**: LSTM networks can be trained on a corpus of music data to learn patterns and structures present in musical compositions.

- **Training Process**: LSTM networks are trained using backpropagation through time (BPTT) to minimize the difference between predicted and actual musical sequences.

Example: Here's a basic example of how you can generate music using Long Short-Term Memory (LSTM) networks in Python using TensorFlow/Keras:

```python
import numpy as np
import tensorflow as tf
from tensorflow.keras.layers import LSTM, Dense
from tensorflow.keras.models import Sequential

# Define the sequence length and number of unique notes/chords
sequence_length = 100
num_unique_notes = 128  # Adjust this according to your music data

# Load and preprocess your music data
# (Assuming you have a dataset of music sequences represented as numpy arrays)
# X_train, y_train = load_and_preprocess_data()

# Define the LSTM model
model = Sequential([
    LSTM(128, input_shape=(sequence_length, num_unique_notes), return_sequences=True),
    LSTM(128),
    Dense(num_unique_notes, activation='softmax')
])

# Compile the model
model.compile(loss='categorical_crossentropy', optimizer='adam')

# Train the model
# model.fit(X_train, y_train, batch_size=64, epochs=100)

# Generate music
def generate_music(model, sequence_length=100, num_notes_to_generate=1000):
```

```python
# Start with a random sequence as input
start_sequence = np.random.randint(0, num_unique_notes, (1, sequence_length, num_unique_notes))
generated_music = []
current_sequence = start_sequence

# Generate notes/chords one at a time
for _ in range(num_notes_to_generate):
    # Predict the next note/chord
    predicted_notes = model.predict(current_sequence, verbose=0)[0]
    # Sample from the predicted probabilities to get the next note/chord
    next_note_index = np.random.choice(range(num_unique_notes), p=predicted_notes)
    next_note = np.zeros(num_unique_notes)
    next_note[next_note_index] = 1
    generated_music.append(next_note)
    # Update the current sequence with the new note/chord
    current_sequence = np.append(current_sequence[:,1:,:], np.expand_dims(next_note, axis=0), axis=1)

return generated_music

# Generate music sequence
generated_sequence = generate_music(model)

# Post-processing (e.g., convert one-hot encoding to MIDI format)
# post_process_and_save(generated_sequence)
```

In this code:

- We define an LSTM model with two LSTM layers and a Dense output layer.

- The model is compiled with categorical cross-entropy loss and the Adam optimizer.

- We generate music by predicting the next note/chord in the sequence based on the previous notes/chords.

- The **generate_music()** function takes the trained model and generates a new music sequence.

- Finally, you would need to implement post-processing to convert the generated sequence into a format suitable for listening or further analysis (e.g., converting one-hot encoded notes/chords to MIDI format).

- Make sure to adjust the model architecture, data preprocessing, and post-processing steps according to the specifics of your music data and requirements.

3. **Music Generation with VAEs:**

    - **Architecture**: VAEs consist of an encoder network that maps input music sequences to a latent space and a decoder network that generates new music samples from latent space.

Training Process: VAEs are trained using variational inference techniques to optimize the parameters of the encoder and decoder networks.

```
import numpy as np
import tensorflow as tf
from tensorflow.keras.layers import Input, Dense, Lambda
from tensorflow.keras.models import Model
from tensorflow.keras.losses import MeanSquaredError
from tensorflow.keras.optimizers import Adam

# Define the parameters
input_shape = (num_features,)   # Adjust according to your music data format
latent_dim = 100
batch_size = 64
num_epochs = 100

# Define the encoder model
inputs = Input(shape=input_shape)
hidden = Dense(512, activation='relu')(inputs)
z_mean = Dense(latent_dim)(hidden)
z_log_var = Dense(latent_dim)(hidden)
```

```python
# Sampling function to sample from the latent space
def sampling(args):
    z_mean, z_log_var = args
    epsilon = tf.random.normal(shape=(tf.shape(z_mean)[0], latent_dim), mean=0.0, stddev=1.0)
    return z_mean + tf.exp(0.5 * z_log_var) * epsilon

z = Lambda(sampling, output_shape=(latent_dim,))([z_mean, z_log_var])

# Define the decoder model
decoder_hidden = Dense(512, activation='relu')(z)
outputs = Dense(num_features, activation='sigmoid')(decoder_hidden)

# Define the VAE model
vae = Model(inputs, outputs)

# Define the loss function
mse_loss = MeanSquaredError()
kl_loss = -0.5 * tf.reduce_mean(1 + z_log_var - tf.square(z_mean) - tf.exp(z_log_var))
vae_loss = mse_loss(inputs, outputs) + kl_loss

# Compile the VAE model
vae.add_loss(vae_loss)
vae.compile(optimizer=Adam(lr=0.001))

# Train the VAE model
#   vae.fit(X_train, X_train, batch_size=batch_size, epochs=num_epochs)

# Generate music samples from the latent space
def generate_music_samples(vae, num_samples=10):
    latent_samples = np.random.normal(0, 1, (num_samples, latent_dim))
    generated_music = vae.predict(latent_samples)
    return generated_music

# Generated music samples
# generated_music = generate_music_samples(vae)
```

In this code:

- We define an encoder model that takes music data as input and outputs the mean and log variance of the latent space.
- We use a sampling function to sample from the latent space based on the mean and log variance.
- We define a decoder model that takes samples from the latent space and reconstructs the music data.
- We define the VAE model by combining the encoder and decoder.
- We define the loss function, which consists of a reconstruction loss (mean squared error) and a KL divergence loss.
- We compile the VAE model and train it on the music data.
- Finally, we generate music samples by sampling from the latent space and decoding them using the VAE model.

Make sure to adjust the model architecture, input/output shapes, and hyperparameters according to the specifics of your music data and requirements.

By leveraging the power of deep learning techniques such as LSTM networks and VAEs, practitioners can create sophisticated models capable of generating new and innovative musical compositions. These models have the potential to revolutionize the way music is composed, produced, and enjoyed in the digital age.

WaveGAN and SpecGAN: Audio Synthesis

WaveGAN and SpecGAN are two generative adversarial network (GAN) architectures specifically designed for audio synthesis. Here's a brief overview of each:

1. **WaveGAN**:

    - **Definition**: WaveGAN is a GAN architecture proposed for generating raw waveform audio samples directly in the time domain.

- **Architecture**: WaveGAN typically consists of a generator network that takes random noise as input and generates raw audio waveforms, and a discriminator network that distinguishes between real and generated audio samples.

- **Training**: WaveGAN is trained using adversarial training, where the generator tries to generate realistic audio samples that can fool the discriminator, while the discriminator aims to distinguish between real and fake audio samples.

- **Loss Function**: The loss function used in WaveGAN typically includes a binary cross-entropy loss for the discriminator and a generator loss that encourages the generated samples to be classified as real by the discriminator.

- **Applications**: WaveGAN can be used for various audio synthesis tasks, including music generation, speech synthesis, and sound effects generation.

Example: Here's a simplified example of how you could implement WaveGAN for audio synthesis using Python and TensorFlow:

```
import numpy as np
import tensorflow as tf
from tensorflow.keras.layers import Conv1D, Flatten, Dense, Reshape
from tensorflow.keras.models import Sequential
from tensorflow.keras.optimizers import Adam

# Define the parameters
num_samples = 16000   # Number of audio samples per waveform (1 second at 16 kHz)
latent_dim = 100  # Latent dimension for the generator input noise
input_shape = (num_samples, 1)  # Input shape for the discriminator

# Generator model
```

```python
generator = Sequential([
    Dense(256, input_dim=latent_dim),
    Conv1D(256, kernel_size=25, strides=4, padding='same', activation='relu'),
    Conv1D(128, kernel_size=25, strides=4, padding='same', activation='relu'),
    Conv1D(64, kernel_size=25, strides=4, padding='same', activation='relu'),
    Conv1D(1, kernel_size=25, strides=4, padding='same', activation='tanh')
])

# Discriminator model
discriminator = Sequential([
    Conv1D(64, kernel_size=25, strides=4, padding='same', input_shape=input_shape),
    Conv1D(128, kernel_size=25, strides=4, padding='same', activation='relu'),
    Conv1D(256, kernel_size=25, strides=4, padding='same', activation='relu'),
    Conv1D(512, kernel_size=25, strides=4, padding='same', activation='relu'),
    Flatten(),
    Dense(1, activation='sigmoid')
])

# Combined model (GAN)
discriminator.compile(optimizer=Adam(lr=0.0002, beta_1=0.5), loss='binary_crossentropy')
discriminator.trainable = False
gan_input = tf.keras.Input(shape=(latent_dim,))
generated_audio = generator(gan_input)
gan_output = discriminator(generated_audio)
gan = tf.keras.Model(gan_input, gan_output)
gan.compile(optimizer=Adam(lr=0.0002, beta_1=0.5), loss='binary_crossentropy')

# Training loop
# Note: You'll need a dataset of real audio waveforms to train WaveGAN.
# Implement the training loop using your dataset and the models defined above.
```

This code sets up the basic architecture for WaveGAN, including the generator and discriminator networks. The next step would be to implement the training loop using a dataset of real audio waveforms. During training, the generator learns to generate realistic audio waveforms that can fool the discriminator, while the discriminator learns to distinguish between real and fake audio waveforms. The combined model (GAN) is then trained to optimize both the generator and discriminator simultaneously. Adjustments and improvements can be made to the architecture and hyperparameters based on the specific requirements of your task and dataset.

2. **SpecGAN** (Spectral GAN):

    - **Definition**: SpecGAN is a GAN architecture designed for audio synthesis in the spectral domain.

    - **Architecture**: SpecGAN operates on the spectrogram representation of audio signals, which provides a time-frequency representation of the audio. It typically consists of a generator network that generates spectrogram frames from random noise, and a discriminator network that distinguishes between real and generated spectrogram frames.

    - **Training**: Similar to WaveGAN, SpecGAN is trained using adversarial training, where the generator aims to generate realistic spectrogram frames that can fool the discriminator, and the discriminator aims to distinguish between real and fake spectrogram frames.

    - **Loss Function**: The loss function used in SpecGAN is similar to WaveGAN, including binary cross-entropy loss for the discriminator and a generator loss that encourages the generated spectrogram frames to be classified as real by the discriminator.

    - **Applications**: SpecGAN can be used for tasks such as music generation, voice conversion, and audio style transfer.

Example: SpaceGAN is a recent advancement in audio synthesis, introduced by researchers to generate diverse and high-quality audio samples. Implementing SpaceGAN from scratch can be complex due to its architectural intricacies. Below is a simplified example of how you could implement SpaceGAN for audio synthesis using Python and TensorFlow:

```python
import numpy as np
import tensorflow as tf
from tensorflow.keras.layers import Conv1D, Flatten, Dense, Reshape, Conv1DTranspose
from tensorflow.keras.models import Sequential
from tensorflow.keras.optimizers import Adam

# Define the parameters
num_samples = 16000  # Number of audio samples per waveform (1 second at 16 kHz)
latent_dim = 100  # Latent dimension for the generator input noise
input_shape = (num_samples, 1)  # Input shape for the discriminator

# Generator model
generator = Sequential([
    Dense(256, input_dim=latent_dim),
    Reshape((1, 256)),
    Conv1DTranspose(128, kernel_size=25, strides=4, padding='same', activation='relu'),
    Conv1DTranspose(64, kernel_size=25, strides=4, padding='same', activation='relu'),
    Conv1DTranspose(1, kernel_size=25, strides=4, padding='same', activation='tanh')
])

# Discriminator model
discriminator = Sequential([
    Conv1D(64, kernel_size=25, strides=4, padding='same', input_shape=input_shape),
    Conv1D(128, kernel_size=25, strides=4, padding='same', activation='relu'),
    Conv1D(256, kernel_size=25, strides=4, padding='same', activation='relu'),
    Conv1D(512, kernel_size=25, strides=4, padding='same', activation='relu'),
    Flatten(),
    Dense(1, activation='sigmoid')
])
```

```
# Combined model (GAN)
discriminator.compile(optimizer=Adam(lr=0.0002, beta_1=0.5), loss='binary_crossentropy')
discriminator.trainable = False
gan_input = tf.keras.Input(shape=(latent_dim,))
generated_audio = generator(gan_input)
gan_output = discriminator(generated_audio)
gan = tf.keras.Model(gan_input, gan_output)
gan.compile(optimizer=Adam(lr=0.0002, beta_1=0.5), loss='binary_crossentropy')

# Training loop
# Note: You'll need a dataset of real audio waveforms to train SpaceGAN.
# Implement the training loop using your dataset and the models defined above.
```

This code sets up the basic architecture for SpaceGAN, including the generator and discriminator networks. The training loop is not provided as it depends on the dataset you have and the specifics of your task. During training, the generator learns to generate realistic audio waveforms that can fool the discriminator, while the discriminator learns to distinguish between real and fake audio waveforms. Adjustments and improvements can be made to the architecture and hyperparameters based on the specific requirements of your task and dataset.

Both WaveGAN and SpecGAN have shown promising results in generating realistic audio samples across various domains. Researchers continue to explore and improve upon these architectures for better audio synthesis capabilities.

Voice Conversion and Speech Synthesis

Voice conversion and speech synthesis are two distinct tasks within the field of generative AI:

1. **Voice Conversion**:

- **Definition**: Voice conversion refers to the process of modifying the speech characteristics of a source speaker to make it sound as if it were spoken by a target speaker, while preserving the linguistic content and overall prosody of the speech.

- **Approach**: Voice conversion models typically learn a mapping between the acoustic features of the source and target speakers' speech signals. This mapping can be learned using various techniques such as Gaussian Mixture Models (GMMs), deep neural networks (DNNs), or more advanced methods like Variational Autoencoders (VAEs) or Generative Adversarial Networks (GANs).

- **Applications**: Voice conversion has applications in telecommunications, entertainment, and human-computer interaction. It can be used to personalize synthetic speech for individuals with speech impairments, dubbing in movies, or creating voice avatars for virtual assistants.

Example: Voice conversion using generative AI typically involves training a model to convert the voice characteristics of a source speaker to those of a target speaker. Here's a simplified example of how you could implement voice conversion using a generative adversarial network (GAN) in Python with TensorFlow:

```
import numpy as np
import tensorflow as tf
from tensorflow.keras.layers import Conv1D, Flatten, Dense, Reshape, Conv1DTranspose
from tensorflow.keras.models import Sequential
from tensorflow.keras.optimizers import Adam

# Define the parameters
num_samples = 16000   # Number of audio samples per waveform (1 second at 16 kHz)
latent_dim = 100 # Latent dimension for the generator input noise
input_shape = (num_samples, 1)   # Input shape for the discriminator
```

```python
# Generator model
generator = Sequential([
    Dense(256, input_dim=latent_dim),
    Reshape((1, 256)),
    Conv1DTranspose(128, kernel_size=25, strides=4, padding='same', activation='relu'),
    Conv1DTranspose(64, kernel_size=25, strides=4, padding='same', activation='relu'),
    Conv1DTranspose(1, kernel_size=25, strides=4, padding='same', activation='tanh')
])

# Discriminator model
discriminator = Sequential([
    Conv1D(64, kernel_size=25, strides=4, padding='same', input_shape=input_shape),
    Conv1D(128, kernel_size=25, strides=4, padding='same', activation='relu'),
    Conv1D(256, kernel_size=25, strides=4, padding='same', activation='relu'),
    Conv1D(512, kernel_size=25, strides=4, padding='same', activation='relu'),
    Flatten(),
    Dense(1, activation='sigmoid')
])

# Combined model (GAN)
discriminator.compile(optimizer=Adam(lr=0.0002, beta_1=0.5), loss='binary_crossentropy')
discriminator.trainable = False
gan_input = tf.keras.Input(shape=(latent_dim,))
generated_audio = generator(gan_input)
gan_output = discriminator(generated_audio)
gan = tf.keras.Model(gan_input, gan_output)
gan.compile(optimizer=Adam(lr=0.0002, beta_1=0.5), loss='binary_crossentropy')

# Training loop
# Note: You'll need a dataset of real audio waveforms to train the voice conversion model.
# Implement the training loop using your dataset and the models defined above.
```

This code sets up the basic architecture for voice conversion using a GAN. During training, the generator learns to convert the voice characteristics of a source speaker to those of a target speaker, while the discriminator learns to distinguish between real and converted audio waveforms. Adjustments and improvements can be made to the architecture and hyperparameters based on the specific requirements of your task and dataset.

2. **Speech Synthesis**:

- **Definition**: Speech synthesis, also known as text-to-speech (TTS) synthesis, refers to the process of generating artificial speech from text input. The goal is to produce natural-sounding speech that conveys the intended meaning of the text.

- **Approach**: Speech synthesis models can be based on concatenative synthesis, where pre-recorded speech segments are concatenated to form the output, or on parametric synthesis, where speech is generated based on statistical models of speech production. Modern approaches to speech synthesis often involve deep learning models such as WaveNet or Tacotron, which directly generate speech waveforms from input text.

- **Applications**: Speech synthesis has a wide range of applications, including voice assistants, navigation systems, audiobooks, and accessibility tools for visually impaired individuals.

- **Example**: Speech synthesis using generative AI typically involves training a model to generate artificial speech from input text. Here's a simplified example of how you could implement speech synthesis using a text-to-speech (TTS) model in Python with TensorFlow:

```
import numpy as np
import tensorflow as tf
from tensorflow.keras.layers import Conv1D, Flatten, Dense, Reshape, Conv1DTranspose
from tensorflow.keras.models import Sequential
from tensorflow.keras.optimizers import Adam
```

```python
# Define the parameters
num_samples = 16000  # Number of audio samples per waveform (1 second at 16 kHz)
input_dim = 100  # Dimension of the input text embedding
input_shape = (input_dim, 1)  # Input shape for the generator

# Generator model
generator = Sequential([
    Dense(256, input_dim=input_dim),
    Reshape((1, 256)),
    Conv1DTranspose(128, kernel_size=25, strides=4, padding='same', activation='relu'),
    Conv1DTranspose(64, kernel_size=25, strides=4, padding='same', activation='relu'),
    Conv1DTranspose(1, kernel_size=25, strides=4, padding='same', activation='tanh')
])

# Compile the generator
generator.compile(optimizer=Adam(lr=0.0002, beta_1=0.5), loss='mse')

# Generate speech from text input
def generate_speech(text_input):
    # Encode text input into a fixed-length embedding
    text_embedding = np.random.randn(input_dim)  # Replace with actual text embedding

    # Generate speech waveform from text embedding
    speech_waveform = generator.predict(text_embedding.reshape(input_shape))[0]

    return speech_waveform

# Example usage
text_input = "Hello, how are you?"
speech_waveform = generate_speech(text_input)
```

This code sets up a basic architecture for speech synthesis using a generative model. In this example, the generator learns to map text embeddings to speech waveforms. During training, the generator learns to generate speech waveforms that correspond to the input text embeddings. Adjustments and improvements can be made to the architecture and hyperparameters based on the specific requirements of your task and dataset. Additionally, you'll need a dataset of text-to-speech pairs to train the model effectively.

In the context of generative AI, both voice conversion and speech synthesis are active areas of research, with ongoing efforts to improve the quality, naturalness, and flexibility of synthesized speech. These technologies play a crucial role in enabling more natural and engaging interactions between humans and machines.

Chapter-8 Ethical and Societal Implications of Generative AI

Deepfakes and Synthetic Media

Deepfakes and synthetic media refer to the use of artificial intelligence (AI) and machine learning techniques to create highly realistic and often deceptive digital content, such as images, videos, and audio recordings. These technologies have the ability to generate convincing fake content that can be difficult to distinguish from authentic media.
Here's a more detailed description of both:

1. **Deepfakes**:

    - **Definition**: Deepfakes are a specific type of synthetic media that use deep learning algorithms, particularly generative adversarial networks (GANs) and autoencoders, to replace a person's likeness in an existing image or video with someone else's. The term "deepfake" is a portmanteau of "deep learning" and "fake."

    - **Creation Process**: Deepfakes are created by training a machine learning model on large datasets of images and videos featuring the target person's face. The model learns to generate new images or videos that convincingly mimic the target person's facial expressions, movements, and speech patterns.

- **Applications**: Deepfakes have been used for various purposes, including entertainment, satire, and political propaganda. However, they have also raised concerns about the potential for misuse, such as spreading misinformation, creating non-consensual pornography, and undermining trust in visual media.

Example: Creating a deepfake using generative AI involves training a model to generate realistic images or videos that manipulate the appearance or behavior of a person. Below is a simplified example of how you could create a deepfake using Python with TensorFlow and Keras:

```
import numpy as np
import tensorflow as tf
from tensorflow.keras.layers import Conv2D, Flatten, Dense, Reshape, Conv2DTranspose
from tensorflow.keras.models import Sequential
from tensorflow.keras.optimizers import Adam

# Define the parameters
input_shape = (64, 64, 3)  # Input shape for the generator
latent_dim = 100  # Latent dimension for the generator input noise

# Generator model
generator = Sequential([
    Dense(256, input_dim=latent_dim),
    Reshape((4, 4, 16)),
    Conv2DTranspose(128, kernel_size=4, strides=2, padding='same', activation='relu'),
    Conv2DTranspose(64, kernel_size=4, strides=2, padding='same', activation='relu'),
    Conv2DTranspose(3, kernel_size=4, strides=2, padding='same', activation='sigmoid')
])

# Compile the generator
generator.compile(optimizer=Adam(lr=0.0002, beta_1=0.5), loss='binary_crossentropy')

# Generate a deepfake image
```

```
def generate_deepfake():
    # Generate random noise as input for the generator
    noise = np.random.randn(latent_dim)

    # Generate the deepfake image
    deepfake_image = generator.predict(noise.reshape((1, latent_dim)))[0]

    return deepfake_image

# Example usage
deepfake_image = generate_deepfake()
```

This code sets up a basic architecture for generating deepfake images using a generative model. The generator learns to map random noise vectors to realistic-looking images that resemble the target person's appearance. During training, the generator learns to produce images that are visually similar to the target person's face.

It's important to note that creating deepfakes raises ethical concerns and may involve legal implications, particularly when it comes to using someone's likeness without their consent. Always ensure that deepfake technology is used responsibly and ethically.

2. **Synthetic Media**:
    - **Definition**: Synthetic media encompasses a broader category of digitally generated content, including not only deepfakes but also other forms of computer-generated imagery (CGI), audio synthesis, and text generation. Synthetic media can be created using a variety of machine learning techniques, including GANs, variational autoencoders (VAEs), and natural language processing (NLP) models.

    - **Creation Process**: The creation process for synthetic media depends on the specific type of content being generated. For example, image and video synthesis typically involve training GANs on large datasets of visual data, while audio synthesis may use similar techniques applied to spectrogram representations of sound. Text generation can be achieved using language models like GPT (Generative Pre-trained Transformer).

- **Applications**: Synthetic media has diverse applications across industries, including entertainment, advertising, virtual reality, and digital art. It enables the creation of immersive experiences, realistic simulations, and personalized content tailored to individual preferences.

Example: Creating synthetic media using generative AI involves training models to generate realistic content such as images, videos, audio, or text. Below is a simplified example of how you could create synthetic images using Python with TensorFlow and Keras

```
import numpy as np
import tensorflow as tf
from tensorflow.keras.layers import Dense, Reshape, Conv2DTranspose
from tensorflow.keras.models import Sequential
from tensorflow.keras.optimizers import Adam

# Define the parameters
input_dim = 100  # Latent dimension for the generator input noise
image_shape = (64, 64, 3)  # Image shape for the generator output

# Generator model
generator = Sequential([
    Dense(256, input_dim=input_dim),
    Reshape((4, 4, 16)),
    Conv2DTranspose(128, kernel_size=4, strides=2, padding='same', activation='relu'),
    Conv2DTranspose(64, kernel_size=4, strides=2, padding='same', activation='relu'),
    Conv2DTranspose(3, kernel_size=4, strides=2, padding='same', activation='sigmoid')
])

# Compile the generator
generator.compile(optimizer=Adam(lr=0.0002, beta_1=0.5), loss='binary_crossentropy')
```

```
# Generate synthetic images
def generate_synthetic_images(num_images):
    # Generate random noise as input for the generator
    noise = np.random.randn(num_images, input_dim)

    # Generate synthetic images
    synthetic_images = generator.predict(noise)

    return synthetic_images

# Example usage
num_images = 10
synthetic_images = generate_synthetic_images(num_images)
```

This code sets up a basic architecture for generating synthetic images using a generative model. The generator learns to map random noise vectors to realistic-looking images. During training, the generator learns to produce images that resemble the training data distribution.

It's important to note that creating synthetic media raises ethical concerns and may involve legal implications, particularly when it comes to generating content that resembles real people or copyrighted material. Always ensure that synthetic media technology is used responsibly and ethically.

While deepfakes and synthetic media offer exciting possibilities for creativity and innovation, they also pose significant ethical, legal, and societal challenges. These include concerns about privacy, consent, authenticity, and the potential for misuse and manipulation. As these technologies continue to advance, it's important to address these challenges and develop responsible practices for their use and regulation.

Bias and Fairness in Generative Models

Bias and fairness in generative models refer to the potential for these models to produce outputs that reflect or amplify existing biases present in the training data or the model design. Generative models, like any machine learning model, can inadvertently learn and propagate biases present in the data

they were trained on. This can lead to unfair or discriminatory outcomes when generating new data or making decisions based on generated data.
Here's a more detailed explanation of bias and fairness in generative models:

1. **Bias**:
    - **Definition**: Bias in generative models refers to systematic errors or inaccuracies in the model's predictions or outputs that result from the model's reliance on biased training data or flawed model design.

    - **Sources of Bias**: Bias in generative models can arise from various sources, including biased training data, biased model architecture or parameters, and biased objectives or loss functions.

    - **Types of Bias**: There are several types of bias that can manifest in generative models, such as demographic bias (e.g., racial or gender bias), cultural bias, linguistic bias, and socioeconomic bias.

    Eample: Addressing linguistic bias in generative AI involves identifying and mitigating biases present in language models to ensure fair and unbiased generation of text. One approach to mitigate linguistic bias is through debiasing techniques during model training. Here's a simplified example of how you could implement debiasing techniques using Python with TensorFlow and Keras:

```
import numpy as np
import tensorflow as tf
from tensorflow.keras.layers import Dense, Embedding, LSTM
from tensorflow.keras.models import Sequential
from tensorflow.keras.optimizers import Adam

# Define the parameters
vocab_size = 10000  # Vocabulary size
embedding_dim = 100  # Embedding dimension
hidden_units = 128  # Number of LSTM hidden units
sequence_length = 20  # Length of input sequences
num_classes = 2  # Number of classes (biased vs. unbiased)
```

```python
# Define the biased training data
biased_sentences = ["He is a doctor.", "She is a nurse.", "He is strong.", "She is kind."]
biased_labels = [1, 1, 0, 0]  # 1 for biased, 0 for unbiased

# Define the debiased training data
debiased_sentences = ["They are a doctor.", "They are a nurse.", "They are strong.", "They are kind."]
debiased_labels = [0, 0, 0, 0]  # 0 for unbiased

# Combine biased and debiased data
sentences = biased_sentences + debiased_sentences
labels = biased_labels + debiased_labels

# Convert sentences to sequences of indices
tokenizer = tf.keras.preprocessing.text.Tokenizer(num_words=vocab_size)
tokenizer.fit_on_texts(sentences)
sequences = tokenizer.texts_to_sequences(sentences)

# Pad sequences to ensure uniform length
padded_sequences = tf.keras.preprocessing.sequence.pad_sequences(sequences, maxlen=sequence_length)

# Define the model architecture
model = Sequential([
    Embedding(input_dim=vocab_size, output_dim=embedding_dim, input_length=sequence_length),
    LSTM(hidden_units),
    Dense(num_classes, activation='softmax')
])

# Compile the model
model.compile(optimizer=Adam(lr=0.001), loss='sparse_categorical_crossentropy', metrics=['accuracy'])

# Train the model
model.fit(padded_sequences, labels, epochs=10, batch_size=32)

# Generate text using the debiased model
def generate_text(seed_text, num_words):
    seed_sequence = tokenizer.texts_to_sequences([seed_text])
```

```
    padded_sequence                              =
tf.keras.preprocessing.sequence.pad_sequences(seed_seque
nce, maxlen=sequence_length)
    predictions = model.predict(padded_sequence)[0]
    predicted_class = np.argmax(predictions)
    return "Biased" if predicted_class == 1 else "Unbiased"

# Example usage
seed_text = "He is"
generated_text = generate_text(seed_text, num_words=1)
print(f"The    model    predicts    that    '{seed_text}'    is
{generated_text}.")
```

This code sets up a simple LSTM-based model to classify text as biased or unbiased based on the training data provided. The biased training data includes sentences with gender bias, while the debiased training data includes neutral sentences. The model is trained on this combined dataset to learn to distinguish between biased and unbiased language. During inference, the model predicts whether a given text input is biased or unbiased. It's important to note that this example is simplified, and real-world debiasing techniques may involve more sophisticated methods and larger datasets. Additionally, evaluating and mitigating linguistic bias in generative AI is an ongoing research area, and there is no one-size-fits-all solution.

2. **Fairness**:

- **Definition**: Fairness in generative models refers to the absence of discriminatory or unfair outcomes in the model's outputs, particularly with respect to sensitive attributes such as race, gender, ethnicity, religion, or socioeconomic status.

- **Fairness Metrics**: Fairness in generative models can be assessed using various fairness metrics and evaluation techniques, such as disparate impact analysis, demographic parity, equal opportunity, and individual fairness.

- **Fairness Constraints**: Fairness constraints can be incorporated into the training process of generative models to mitigate bias and promote fairness in the generated outputs. This may involve modifying the training data, adjusting the model architecture or objective, or applying post-processing techniques to the generated data.

Example: Addressing fairness in generative AI involves implementing techniques to ensure that generated outputs are equitable and unbiased with respect to sensitive attributes such as race, gender, or ethnicity. One approach to promoting fairness is through adversarial training, where an additional discriminator model is trained to classify generated outputs based on fairness criteria. Below is a simplified example of how you could implement fairness in generative AI using adversarial training with Python, TensorFlow, and Keras:

```
import numpy as np
import tensorflow as tf
from tensorflow.keras.layers import Dense, Input
from tensorflow.keras.models import Model
from tensorflow.keras.optimizers import Adam

# Define the parameters
input_dim = 100   # Latent dimension for the generator input noise
output_dim = 1    # Output dimension for the discriminator (fairness classifier)

# Generator model
generator_input = Input(shape=(input_dim,))
generator_output = Dense(64, activation='relu')(generator_input)
generator_output = Dense(64, activation='relu')(generator_output)
generator_output = Dense(output_dim, activation='sigmoid')(generator_output)
generator = Model(generator_input, generator_output)

# Discriminator model (fairness classifier)
discriminator_input = Input(shape=(output_dim,))
discriminator_output = Dense(64, activation='relu')(discriminator_input)
discriminator_output = Dense(64, activation='relu')(discriminator_output)
```

```
discriminator_output = Dense(1,
activation='sigmoid')(discriminator_output)
discriminator = Model(discriminator_input,
discriminator_output)

# Compile the discriminator
discriminator.compile(optimizer=Adam(lr=0.0002),
loss='binary_crossentropy', metrics=['accuracy'])

# Adversarial model (combined generator and discriminator)
adversarial_input = Input(shape=(input_dim,))
adversarial_output =
discriminator(generator(adversarial_input))
adversarial_model = Model(adversarial_input,
adversarial_output)

# Compile the adversarial model
adversarial_model.compile(optimizer=Adam(lr=0.0002),
loss='binary_crossentropy', metrics=['accuracy'])

# Train the adversarial model
def train_adversarial_model(num_iterations):
    for _ in range(num_iterations):
        # Generate random noise as input for the generator
        noise = np.random.randn(32, input_dim)

        # Generate synthetic data using the generator
        synthetic_data = generator.predict(noise)

        # Create labels for the synthetic data (0 for fair, 1 for unfair)
        labels = np.random.randint(2, size=(32, 1))

        # Train the discriminator on the synthetic data
        discriminator.train_on_batch(synthetic_data, labels)

        # Train the adversarial model on the synthetic data
        adversarial_model.train_on_batch(noise, np.ones((32, 1)))

# Example usage
train_adversarial_model(num_iterations=1000)
```

This code sets up a simple adversarial training framework to promote fairness in generative AI. The generator learns to produce synthetic data, while the discriminator (fairness classifier) learns to distinguish between fair and unfair outputs. During training, the adversarial model (combined generator and discriminator) is trained to generate fair outputs that are difficult for the discriminator to classify.

It's important to note that this example is simplified, and real-world fairness techniques may involve more sophisticated methods and evaluation criteria. Additionally, fairness in generative AI is a complex and evolving research area, and there is ongoing work to develop effective techniques for promoting fairness in AI-generated outputs.

Addressing bias and promoting fairness in generative models is essential for ensuring that these models produce equitable and inclusive outcomes. This requires careful consideration of the data used to train the models, the design and implementation of the models themselves, and the evaluation of model performance with respect to fairness criteria. Additionally, ongoing research and development efforts are needed to develop techniques for detecting and mitigating bias in generative models and to promote the responsible and ethical use of these technologies.

Regulation and Responsible Use of Generative AI

Regulation and responsible use of generative AI refer to the legal frameworks, guidelines, and ethical principles established to govern the development, deployment, and application of generative artificial intelligence (AI) technologies. These regulations and principles aim to ensure that generative AI systems are developed and used in a manner that prioritizes ethical considerations, protects human rights, and mitigates potential risks and harms associated with their deployment. Here's a more detailed explanation:

1. **Regulation**:

    - **Definition**: Regulation refers to the process of establishing laws, rules, and policies that govern the development, deployment, and use of generative AI technologies. These regulations may be enacted by governments, regulatory agencies, or international bodies to ensure compliance with legal and ethical standards.

- **Purpose**: The primary purpose of regulation is to safeguard individuals, organizations, and society at large from the potential risks and negative consequences associated with generative AI technologies. Regulation seeks to address concerns such as privacy violations, bias and discrimination, security vulnerabilities, and the misuse of AI-generated content.

2. **Responsible Use**:
    - **Definition**: Responsible use of generative AI involves adhering to ethical principles, best practices, and guidelines to ensure that AI technologies are developed, deployed, and utilized in a manner that is ethical, transparent, and accountable.

    - **Key Principles**: Responsible use principles may include fairness, transparency, accountability, privacy protection, safety, and inclusivity. These principles guide the development and deployment of generative AI systems and help mitigate potential risks and negative impacts.

    - **Stakeholder Engagement**: Responsible use of generative AI requires collaboration and engagement among various stakeholders, including AI developers, researchers, policymakers, businesses, civil society organizations, and affected communities. Stakeholder engagement fosters dialogue, consensus-building, and the development of shared norms and standards for responsible AI use.

3. **Key Considerations**:
    - **Ethical Frameworks**: Developing ethical frameworks and guidelines for the design,

development, and deployment of generative AI systems.

- **Transparency**: Ensuring transparency in AI systems to facilitate understanding, accountability, and trust among users and stakeholders.

- **Accountability**: Establishing mechanisms for accountability and redress in cases of AI-related harm or misuse.

- **Privacy Protection**: Safeguarding individuals' privacy rights and ensuring responsible data handling practices in AI systems.

- **Bias Mitigation**: Addressing bias and discrimination in AI algorithms and data to promote fairness and inclusivity.

- **Safety and Security**: Ensuring the safety, security, and robustness of AI systems to prevent unintended consequences and malicious use.

- **Human-Centric Design**: Prioritizing human well-being, autonomy, and dignity in the design and deployment of AI technologies.

Overall, By adopting ethical principles, adhering to best practices, and engaging with stakeholders, policymakers, and the public, we can promote the responsible and beneficial use of generative AI while mitigating potential risks.

Chapter-9   Large Language Models (LLMs)

Large Language Models (LLMs) are advanced AI systems designed to understand and generate human-like text based on vast amounts of data. They use deep learning techniques, particularly transformers, to process and generate text. LLMs like GPT-3 and GPT-4 from OpenAI, BERT from Google, and others have set new standards in natural language understanding and generation.

Key Features of LLMs

Transformers Architecture: LLMs use transformer models, which rely on self-attention mechanisms to process input data in parallel, making them highly efficient for handling long-range dependencies in text.

Pretraining and Fine-Tuning: These models are typically pretrained on a massive corpus of text data and then fine-tuned on specific tasks to enhance performance.

Contextual Understanding: LLMs can understand and generate text with coherent context, making them suitable for a wide range of applications like text generation, translation, summarization, and question-answering.

Example: Using OpenAI's GPT-3

Below is an example of how to use OpenAI's GPT-3 model in Python using the **openai** library. You need to have an API key from OpenAI to use their GPT-3 model.
Step-by-Step Implementation

Install the OpenAI Python Library

First, ensure you have the OpenAI Python library installed:

pip install openai

Import Required Libraries and Set Up API Key

Import the **openai** library and set your API key:

import openai

# Set your OpenAI API key
openai.api_key = 'your-api-key'

Generate Text Using GPT-3

Use the **openai.Completion.create** method to generate text:

```
def generate_text(prompt, model="text-davinci-003", max_tokens=100):
    response = openai.Completion.create(
        model=model,
        prompt=prompt,
        max_tokens=max_tokens,
        n=1,
        stop=None,
        temperature=0.7
    )
    return response.choices[0].text.strip()

# Example prompt
prompt = "Explain the significance of Large Language Models in AI."

# Generate text
generated_text = generate_text(prompt)
print("Generated Text:\n", generated_text)
```

Output

The output will be a coherent paragraph generated by GPT-3 based on the provided prompt:
Generated Text:
Large Language Models (LLMs) have revolutionized the field of artificial intelligence by demonstrating remarkable capabilities in

understanding and generating human-like text. These models, such as GPT-3, leverage the power of deep learning and vast datasets to process and produce text with high coherence and context awareness. LLMs have numerous applications, including natural language processing, translation, summarization, and more, making them invaluable tools in various industries.

Example: Using Hugging Face's Transformers Library with BERT

Here's how to use the Hugging Face Transformers library to perform a text generation task with a model like GPT-2 (for generation) or BERT (for other NLP tasks):

Install the Transformers Library

Install the Hugging Face Transformers library:

```
pip install transformers
```

Import Required Libraries

Import the necessary libraries and load the model:

```
from transformers import GPT2LMHeadModel, GPT2Tokenizer

# Load pre-trained model and tokenizer

model_name = 'gpt2'
model = GPT2LMHeadModel.from_pretrained(model_name)
tokenizer = GPT2Tokenizer.from_pretrained(model_name)
```

Generate Text Using GPT-2

Generate text using the GPT-2 model:

```
def generate_text_with_gpt2(prompt, max_length=50):
    inputs = tokenizer.encode(prompt, return_tensors='pt')
    outputs = model.generate(inputs, max_length=max_length, num_return_sequences=1)
    return tokenizer.decode(outputs[0], skip_special_tokens=True)

# Example prompt
```

prompt = "The future of AI involves"

# Generate text
generated_text = generate_text_with_gpt2(prompt)
print("Generated Text:\n", generated_text)

Output

The output will be a generated continuation of the provided prompt using GPT-2:

Generated Text:
The future of AI involves creating increasingly sophisticated models that can understand and interact with the world in more complex and nuanced ways. These advancements will likely lead to significant improvements in various fields, from healthcare and education to transportation and entertainment.
Summary
Large Language Models like GPT-3 and BERT represent significant advancements in the field of AI, enabling machines to generate and understand human-like text with high accuracy and contextual relevance. By leveraging transformers and large-scale pretraining, these models have become powerful tools for a wide range of applications in natural language processing.

Fundamentals of Natural Language Processing (NLP)

Basics of NLP: Tokenization, Lemmatization, and Part-of-Speech Tagging

1. **Tokenization:**
   Tokenization is the process of breaking down a text into smaller units called tokens. These tokens can be words, phrases, or characters, depending on the level of granularity required.
   For example, given the sentence "The cat is sleeping", tokenization would produce the tokens: ["The", "cat", "is", "sleeping"].

Tokenization helps in preparing text data for further analysis, such as sentiment analysis, text classification, or language modelling.
here's an example of tokenization in Python using the NLTK library:

```
import nltk
from nltk.tokenize import word_tokenize, sent_tokenize

# Sample text for tokenization
text = "Tokenization is the process of breaking down text into smaller units called tokens. These tokens can be words, phrases, or characters."

# Tokenize the text into words
words = word_tokenize(text)
print("Word tokens:", words)

# Tokenize the text into sentences
sentences = sent_tokenize(text)
print("Sentence tokens:", sentences)
```

This code imports the NLTK library and specifically the **word_tokenize** and **sent_tokenize** functions for tokenizing words and sentences, respectively. It then tokenizes a sample text into words and sentences and prints the tokens.

Make sure you have NLTK installed (**pip install nltk**) and have downloaded the necessary resources by running **nltk.download('punkt')** before executing the code. This will ensure that the tokenization functions work correctly.

2. **Lemmatization:**
Lemmatization is the process of reducing words to their base or dictionary form, called the lemma. It involves removing inflections and variations to standardize words.
For example, the lemma of the word "running" is "run", and the lemma of "went" is "go".
Lemmatization helps in reducing the dimensionality of text data and improving the accuracy of downstream NLP tasks by treating different forms of a word as the same.

here's an example of lemmatization in Python using the NLTK library:

```
import nltk
from nltk.stem import WordNetLemmatizer

# Initialize the WordNet lemmatizer
lemmatizer = WordNetLemmatizer()

# Sample text for lemmatization
text = "The cats are running and jumping around the house"

# Tokenize the text into words
words = nltk.word_tokenize(text)

# Lemmatize each word in the text
lemmatized_words = [lemmatizer.lemmatize(word) for word in words]

print("Original words:", words)
print("Lemmatized words:", lemmatized_words)
```

In this code:

- We import the NLTK library and specifically the **WordNetLemmatizer** class for lemmatization.

- We initialize a WordNet lemmatizer object.

- We define a sample text to be lemmatized.

- We tokenize the text into individual words using the **word_tokenize** function from NLTK.

- We then lemmatize each word in the text using the **lemmatize** method of the lemmatizer object.

- Finally, we print the original words and their corresponding lemmatized forms.

Make sure you have NLTK installed (**pip install nltk**) and have downloaded the necessary resources by running **nltk.download('punkt')** and **nltk.download('wordnet')** before executing the code. This will ensure that the tokenization and lemmatization functions work correctly.

Part-of-Speech (POS) Tagging:

Part-of-Speech tagging is the process of assigning grammatical tags to words in a sentence based on their syntactic function and role.
Common POS tags include nouns, verbs, adjectives, adverbs, pronouns, prepositions, conjunctions, and interjections.
For example, in the sentence "The cat is sleeping", POS tagging would produce the tags: [("The", "DT"), ("cat", "NN"), ("is", "VBZ"), ("sleeping", "VBG")].
POS tagging helps in understanding the grammatical structure of sentences and is used in various NLP tasks such as named entity recognition, syntactic parsing, and text generation.

here's an example of Part-of-Speech (POS) tagging in Python using the NLTK library:

```
import nltk

# Sample text for POS tagging
text = "The quick brown fox jumps over the lazy dog"

# Tokenize the text into words
words = nltk.word_tokenize(text)

# Perform POS tagging
pos_tags = nltk.pos_tag(words)

print("Word tokens:", words)
print("POS tags:", pos_tags)
```

In this code:

- We import the NLTK library.

- We define a sample text to be POS tagged.

- We tokenize the text into individual words using the **word_tokenize** function from NLTK.

- We then perform POS tagging on the words using the **pos_tag** function from NLTK, which assigns a POS tag to each word based on its grammatical role.

- Finally, we print the original words and their corresponding POS tags.

- Make sure you have NLTK installed (**pip install nltk**) and have downloaded the necessary resources by running **nltk.download('punkt')** and **nltk.download('averaged_perceptron_tagger')** before executing the code. This will ensure that the tokenization and POS tagging functions work correctly.

In practice, tokenization, lemmatization, and POS tagging are often performed as pre-processing steps before further analysis or processing of text data. These techniques help in standardizing and structuring text data, making it easier for machines to understand and analyse natural language text.

Python libraries such as NLTK (Natural Language Toolkit), spaCy, and TextBlob provide built-in functions and tools for performing tokenization, lemmatization, and POS tagging, making it easy to incorporate these techniques into NLP workflows.

Word Embeddings: Word2Vec, GloVe, and FastText

Word2Vec:

Word2Vec is a popular word embedding technique developed by researchers at Google. It represents words as dense vectors in a continuous vector space, where similar words have similar vector representations.

Word2Vec consists of two main models: Continuous Bag of Words (CBOW) and Skip-gram. CBOW predicts a target word based on its context words, while Skip-gram predicts context words given a target word.

The Word2Vec model is trained on large text corpora using shallow neural networks, which learn to predict the surrounding words based on the input word or vice versa.

Word2Vec embeddings capture semantic relationships between words and are commonly used in various NLP tasks such as sentiment analysis, named entity recognition, and machine translation.

Here's an example of how to train a Word2Vec model using the Gensim library in Python:

```python
from gensim.models import Word2Vec
from nltk.tokenize import word_tokenize

# Sample corpus
corpus = [
    "the quick brown fox jumps over the lazy dog",
    "he is walking in the park",
    "she loves to read books"
]

# Tokenize the corpus
tokenized_corpus = [word_tokenize(sentence.lower()) for sentence in corpus]

# Train the Word2Vec model
model = Word2Vec(sentences=tokenized_corpus, vector_size=100, window=5, min_count=1, workers=4)

# Get the word vectors
word_vectors = model.wv

# Find similar words
similar_words = word_vectors.most_similar("dog")

print("Similar words to 'dog':", similar_words)
```

In this code:
- We import the Word2Vec class from the Gensim library and the **word_tokenize** function from NLTK for tokenization.
- We define a sample corpus containing three sentences.
- We tokenize the corpus into words.
- We train the Word2Vec model using the tokenized corpus. Here, **vector_size** specifies the dimensionality of the word vectors, **window** specifies the maximum distance between the current and predicted word within a sentence, **min_count** specifies the minimum frequency of a word to be included in the model, and **workers** specifies the number of CPU cores to use for training.
- We obtain the word vectors from the trained model.
- Finally, we find similar words to the word "dog" using the **most_similar** method of the **word_vectors** object.

Make sure you have Gensim and NLTK installed (**pip install gensim nltk**) and have downloaded the necessary resources by running **nltk.download('punkt')** before executing the code. This will ensure that the tokenization and Word2Vec model training work correctly.

GloVe (Global Vectors for Word Representation):

- GloVe is another popular word embedding technique developed by researchers at Stanford University. It learns word embeddings by factorizing the co-occurrence matrix of words in a corpus.
- GloVe embeddings capture global word co-occurrence statistics, representing words based on their distributional properties across the entire corpus.
- Unlike Word2Vec, GloVe embeddings are pre-trained on large corpora such as Wikipedia or Common Crawl and are available in pre-trained models of various dimensions.
- GloVe embeddings are widely used in NLP tasks, particularly in scenarios where capturing global semantic relationships between words is important.

To use GloVe in Python, you can either train your own embeddings or use pre-trained embeddings. Here's an example of how to use pre-trained GloVe embeddings with the **glove-python** library:

First, install the library using pip:

pip install glove-python-binary

Then, you can use the pre-trained embeddings in your Python code as follows:

from glove import Corpus, Glove

```
# Sample corpus
corpus = [
    "the quick brown fox jumps over the lazy dog",
    "he is walking in the park",
    "she loves to read books"
```

]

```
# Tokenize the corpus
tokenized_corpus = [sentence.lower().split() for sentence in corpus]

# Train the GloVe model
corpus_model = Corpus()
corpus_model.fit(tokenized_corpus, window=5)

glove = Glove(no_components=100, learning_rate=0.05)
glove.fit(corpus_model.matrix, epochs=100, no_threads=4, verbose=True)
glove.add_dictionary(corpus_model.dictionary)

# Get the word vectors
word_vectors = glove.word_vectors

# Find similar words
similar_words = glove.most_similar("dog", number=5)

print("Similar words to 'dog':", similar_words)
```

In this code:

- We import the **Corpus** and **Glove** classes from the **glove** module.
- We define a sample corpus containing three sentences.
- We tokenize the corpus into words.
- We train the GloVe model using the tokenized corpus.
- We obtain the word vectors from the trained model.
- Finally, we find similar words to the word "dog" using the **most_similar** method of the **glove** object.

Make sure you have the necessary resources for NLTK tokenization and the **glove-python-binary** library installed before executing the code. Additionally, you may need to download pre-trained GloVe word vectors from the GloVe website and load them using the **Glove.load_stanford** method if you want to use pre-trained embeddings.

FastText:

- FastText is an extension of Word2Vec developed by Facebook AI Research. It represents words as bags of character n-grams, enabling it to capture subword information and handle out-of-vocabulary words more effectively.

- FastText embeddings are trained using a hierarchical softmax or negative sampling approach, similar to Word2Vec.

- In addition to word embeddings, FastText also supports subword embeddings, which allow it to represent unseen words by averaging the embeddings of their character n-grams.

- FastText embeddings are particularly useful for handling morphologically rich languages, rare words, and misspellings, and are widely used in applications like text classification, information retrieval, and language modeling.

Here's an example of how to use FastText in Python using the **gensim** library:
First, install the library using pip:
pip install genism

Then, you can use FastText in your Python code as follows:

```
from gensim.models import FastText
from nltk.tokenize import word_tokenize

# Sample corpus
corpus = [
    "the quick brown fox jumps over the lazy dog",
    "he is walking in the park",
    "she loves to read books"
]

# Tokenize the corpus
tokenized_corpus = [word_tokenize(sentence.lower()) for sentence in corpus]
```

```
# Train the FastText model
model = FastText(sentences=tokenized_corpus, vector_size=100, window=5, min_count=1, workers=4)

# Get the word vectors
word_vectors = model.wv

# Find similar words
similar_words = word_vectors.most_similar("dog")

print("Similar words to 'dog':", similar_words)
```

In this code:

- We import the **FastText** class from the **gensim.models** module and the **word_tokenize** function from NLTK for tokenization.

- We define a sample corpus containing three sentences.

- We tokenize the corpus into words.
- We train the FastText model using the tokenized corpus. Here, **vector_size** specifies the dimensionality of the word vectors, **window** specifies the maximum distance between the current and predicted word within a sentence, **min_count** specifies the minimum frequency of a word to be included in the model, and **workers** specifies the number of CPU cores to use for training.

- We obtain the word vectors from the trained model.

- Finally, we find similar words to the word "dog" using the **most_similar** method of the **word_vectors** object.

Make sure you have NLTK installed (**pip install nltk**) and have downloaded the necessary resources by running **nltk.download('punkt')** before executing the code. This will ensure that the tokenization and FastText model training work correctly.

Each of these word embedding techniques has its strengths and weaknesses, and the choice of embedding method depends on the specific requirements of the NLP task and the characteristics of the text data. Researchers and practitioners often experiment with multiple embedding techniques to find the most suitable representation for their applications.

Variants of Transformers: BERT, GPT, T5, XLNet, etc.

Variants of Transformers have pushed the boundaries of natural language processing and have been pivotal in achieving state-of-the-art results in various tasks. Here's an overview of some prominent variants:

1. BERT (Bidirectional Encoder Representations from Transformers):

- BERT introduced the concept of bidirectional pre-training for language representations.
- It is pre-trained on large corpora using masked language modeling and next sentence prediction tasks.
- BERT has achieved state-of-the-art results on a wide range of NLP tasks, including question answering, sentiment analysis, and named entity recognition.

Below is a simple example of how you can use the pre-trained BERT model for text classification using the transformers library in Python:

```
import torch
from transformers import BertTokenizer, BertForSequenceClassification
from torch.utils.data import DataLoader
from torch.utils.data import TensorDataset

# Load pre-trained BERT model and tokenizer
model_name = 'bert-base-uncased'
tokenizer = BertTokenizer.from_pretrained(model_name)
```

```python
model = BertForSequenceClassification.from_pretrained(model_name)

# Example text for classification
text = "This is a positive review."

# Tokenize input text
inputs = tokenizer(text, return_tensors="pt")

# Perform classification
outputs = model(**inputs)

# Get predicted label
predicted_class = torch.argmax(outputs.logits, dim=1).item()

# Decode predicted label
label_list = ["negative", "positive"] # Example label list
predicted_label = label_list[predicted_class]

print("Predicted label:", predicted_label)
```

In this code:

- We import necessary libraries including **torch** and **transformers**.

- We load the pre-trained BERT model and tokenizer using the **BertTokenizer** and **BertForSequenceClassification** classes from the **transformers** library.

- We define an example text for classification.

- We tokenize the input text using the tokenizer.

- We pass the tokenized input to the BERT model and obtain the model's outputs, including the logits for each class.

- We extract the predicted class label by taking the argmax of the logits.

- We decode the predicted class label using a label list.

- Finally, we print the predicted label.

This code demonstrates a basic text classification task using the pre-trained BERT model. You can fine-tune this model on your specific dataset for more accurate predictions. Additionally, you may need to adjust the input data format and labels according to your dataset.

2. **GPT (Generative Pre-trained Transformer):**

    - GPT is a series of models developed by OpenAI that use a left-to-right architecture for pre-training.

    - It is trained on large text corpora using a causal language modeling objective, where the model predicts the next token in a sequence given the previous tokens.

    - GPT has demonstrated impressive performance in tasks such as text generation, language translation, and summarization.

Here's a simple example of how to generate text using the pre-trained GPT-2 model in Python using the transformers library:

```
import torch
from transformers import GPT2LMHeadModel, GPT2Tokenizer

# Load pre-trained GPT-2 model and tokenizer
model_name = "gpt2-medium"
tokenizer = GPT2Tokenizer.from_pretrained(model_name)
model = GPT2LMHeadModel.from_pretrained(model_name)

# Set the model to evaluation mode
model.eval()

# Generate text
input_text = "Once upon a time"
input_ids = tokenizer.encode(input_text, return_tensors='pt')
output = model.generate(input_ids, max_length=100, num_return_sequences=1, temperature=0.7)

# Decode generated text
generated_text = tokenizer.decode(output[0], skip_special_tokens=True)
```

print("Generated text:", generated_text)

In this code:

- We import necessary libraries including **torch** and **transformers**.

- We load the pre-trained GPT-2 model and tokenizer using the **GPT2LMHeadModel** and **GPT2Tokenizer** classes from the **transformers** library.

- We set the model to evaluation mode using **model.eval()**.

- We define an example input text to start the generation process.

- We encode the input text using the tokenizer and pass it to the model's **generate** method to generate text.

- We decode the generated text using the tokenizer.

- Finally, we print the generated text.

You can adjust the **max_length** and **temperature** parameters in the **generate** method to control the length and creativity of the generated text, respectively. Additionally, you can fine-tune the model on your specific dataset for better text generation performance.

3. **T5 (Text-To-Text Transfer Transformer)**:

    - T5 is a transformer model introduced by Google Research that unifies different NLP tasks under a single text-to-text framework.

    - It is trained on a diverse range of tasks by framing each task as a text-to-text problem, where both inputs and outputs are represented as text.

- T5 achieves state-of-the-art results on various benchmarks and provides a unified approach for handling different NLP tasks.

To use the T5 model for text-to-text tasks like summarization, translation, and question answering, you can follow this example using the Hugging Face transformers library:

```python
import torch
from transformers import T5ForConditionalGeneration, T5Tokenizer

# Load pre-trained T5 model and tokenizer
model_name = "t5-small"
tokenizer = T5Tokenizer.from_pretrained(model_name)
model = T5ForConditionalGeneration.from_pretrained(model_name)

# Set the model to evaluation mode
model.eval()

# Example text for summarization
text = "The T5 model is a text-to-text transformer that can be used for various NLP tasks."

# Tokenize input text
input_text = "summarize: " + text
input_ids = tokenizer.encode(input_text, return_tensors="pt")

# Generate summary
output_ids = model.generate(input_ids, max_length=50, num_beams=4, early_stopping=True)

# Decode summary
summary = tokenizer.decode(output_ids[0], skip_special_tokens=True)

print("Generated summary:", summary)
```

This code example summarizes the given input text using a pre-trained T5 model. Here's a breakdown:

- We import the necessary libraries, including **torch** and **transformers**.

- We load the pre-trained T5 model and tokenizer using **T5ForConditionalGeneration** and **T5Tokenizer** classes from the **transformers** library.

- We set the model to evaluation mode using **model.eval()**.

- We define an example input text for summarization.

- We preprocess the input text by adding the task prefix ("summarize:") and tokenizing it using the tokenizer.

- We pass the tokenized input to the model's **generate** method to generate a summary.

- We decode the generated summary using the tokenizer and print it out.

You can similarly modify the code for other text-to-text tasks like translation or question answering by changing the task prefix and input text accordingly. Additionally, you can adjust parameters like **max_length** and **num_beams** to control the length and beam search width during generation, respectively.

4. **XLNet**:

 - XLNet is a transformer model developed by Google AI and CMU that integrates ideas from autoregressive models (like GPT) and autoencoding models (like BERT).

 - It uses a permutation language modeling objective, where the model predicts tokens conditioned on all permutations of the input sequence.

 - XLNet achieves superior performance by capturing bidirectional context while avoiding the limitations of fixed-context autoregressive models.

To use the XLNet model for text generation, classification, or any other task, you can follow this example using the Hugging Face transformers library:

```
import torch
from transformers import XLNetTokenizer, XLNetForSequenceClassification

# Load pre-trained XLNet model and tokenizer
model_name = "xlnet-base-cased"
tokenizer = XLNetTokenizer.from_pretrained(model_name)
model = XLNetForSequenceClassification.from_pretrained(model_name)

# Set the model to evaluation mode
model.eval()

# Example text for classification
text = "This is a positive review."

# Tokenize input text
input_ids = tokenizer.encode(text, add_special_tokens=True, return_tensors="pt")

# Perform classification
with torch.no_grad():
    outputs = model(input_ids)

# Get predicted class
predicted_class = torch.argmax(outputs.logits, dim=1).item()

# Decode predicted class
label_list = ["negative", "positive"]  # Example label list
predicted_label = label_list[predicted_class]

print("Predicted label:", predicted_label)
```

In this example:

- We import the necessary libraries, including **torch** and **transformers**.

- We load the pre-trained XLNet model and tokenizer using the **XLNetTokenizer** and **XLNetForSequenceClassification** classes from the **transformers** library.

- We set the model to evaluation mode using **model.eval()**.

- We define an example input text for classification.

- We tokenize the input text using the tokenizer.

- We pass the tokenized input to the model and obtain the model's outputs, including the logits for each class.

- We extract the predicted class label by taking the argmax of the logits.

- We decode the predicted class label using a label list.

You can adjust this code for other tasks such as text generation or sequence labeling by using different pre-trained XLNet models (**XLNetForSequenceClassification**, **XLNetForTokenClassification**, etc.) and changing the input data format accordingly. Additionally, you may need to adjust the label list according to your dataset.

5. **RoBERTa (Robustly optimized BERT approach)**:

- RoBERTa is a variant of BERT introduced by Facebook AI, which uses dynamic masking during pre-training and larger batch sizes to improve robustness and performance.

- It is trained on a larger corpus for a longer duration compared to BERT and achieves improved performance on various downstream tasks.

To use RoBERTa for text classification, you can follow this example using the Hugging Face transformers library:

import torch

```python
from transformers import RobertaTokenizer, RobertaForSequenceClassification

# Load pre-trained RoBERTa model and tokenizer
model_name = "roberta-base"
tokenizer = RobertaTokenizer.from_pretrained(model_name)
model = RobertaForSequenceClassification.from_pretrained(model_name)

# Set the model to evaluation mode
model.eval()

# Example text for classification
text = "This is a positive review."

# Tokenize input text
inputs = tokenizer(text, return_tensors="pt")

# Perform classification
with torch.no_grad():
    outputs = model(**inputs)

# Get predicted class
predicted_class = torch.argmax(outputs.logits, dim=1).item()

# Decode predicted class
label_list = ["negative", "positive"]  # Example label list
predicted_label = label_list[predicted_class]

print("Predicted label:", predicted_label)
```

In this example:

- We import the necessary libraries, including **torch** and **transformers**.

- We load the pre-trained RoBERTa model and tokenizer using the **RobertaTokenizer** and **RobertaForSequenceClassification** classes from the **transformers** library.

- We set the model to evaluation mode using **model.eval()**.

- We define an example input text for classification.
- We tokenize the input text using the tokenizer.
- We pass the tokenized input to the model and obtain the model's outputs, including the logits for each class.
- We extract the predicted class label by taking the argmax of the logits.
- We decode the predicted class label using a label list.

You can adjust this code for other tasks such as text generation or sequence labeling by using different pre-trained RoBERTa models **(RobertaForSequenceClassification, RobertaForTokenClassification**, etc.) and changing the input data format accordingly. Additionally, you may need to adjust the label list according to your dataset.

6. **DistilBERT**:

    - DistilBERT is a smaller and faster version of BERT introduced by Hugging Face.
    - It retains most of BERT's performance while reducing memory and computational requirements, making it suitable for deployment in resource-constrained environments.

To use DistilBERT for text classification, you can follow this example using the Hugging Face transformers library:

```
import torch
from transformers import DistilBertTokenizer, DistilBertForSequenceClassification

# Load pre-trained DistilBERT model and tokenizer
model_name = "distilbert-base-uncased"
tokenizer = DistilBertTokenizer.from_pretrained(model_name)
model = DistilBertForSequenceClassification.from_pretrained(model_name)
```

```
# Set the model to evaluation mode
model.eval()

# Example text for classification
text = "This is a positive review."

# Tokenize input text
inputs = tokenizer(text, return_tensors="pt")

# Perform classification
with torch.no_grad():
    outputs = model(**inputs)

# Get predicted class
predicted_class = torch.argmax(outputs.logits, dim=1).item()

# Decode predicted class
label_list = ["negative", "positive"] # Example label list
predicted_label = label_list[predicted_class]

print("Predicted label:", predicted_label)
```

In this example:

- We import the necessary libraries, including **torch** and **transformers**.

- We load the pre-trained DistilBERT model and tokenizer using the **DistilBertTokenizer** and **DistilBertForSequenceClassification** classes from the **transformers** library.

- We set the model to evaluation mode using **model.eval()**.

- We define an example input text for classification.

- We tokenize the input text using the tokenizer.

- We pass the tokenized input to the model and obtain the model's outputs, including the logits for each class.

- We extract the predicted class label by taking the argmax of the logits.

- We decode the predicted class label using a label list.

You can adjust this code for other tasks such as text generation or sequence labeling by using different pre-trained DistilBERT models (**DistilBertForSequenceClassification, DistilBertForTokenClassification**, etc.) and changing the input data format accordingly. Additionally, you may need to adjust the label list according to your dataset.

These variants of Transformers have significantly advanced the field of natural language processing, demonstrating the effectiveness of transformer-based architectures in capturing complex linguistic patterns and achieving state-of-the-art performance on various NLP tasks.

Pre-training and Fine-tuning LLMs

Pre-training Objectives: Masked Language Modeling, Next Sentence Prediction

Masked Language Modeling (MLM) and Next Sentence Prediction (NSP) are two pre-training objectives commonly used in transformer-based models like BERT, RoBERTa, and GPT. Here's an overview of each:

1. **Masked Language Modeling (MLM)**:

    - MLM is a pre-training objective where a certain percentage of tokens in the input sequence are randomly masked, and the model is trained to predict the original tokens based on the context.

    - During pre-training, a random subset of tokens in each input sequence is replaced with a special **[MASK]** token.

- The model is then trained to predict the original tokens based on the remaining unmasked tokens and the context provided by surrounding tokens.

- MLM encourages the model to learn bidirectional representations and captures contextual information from both left and right contexts.

Here's a Python code example demonstrating how to perform Masked Language Modeling (MLM) using a pre-trained BERT model and the Hugging Face transformers library:

```
from transformers import BertTokenizer, BertForMaskedLM
import torch

# Load pre-trained BERT model and tokenizer
model_name = "bert-base-uncased"
tokenizer = BertTokenizer.from_pretrained(model_name)
model = BertForMaskedLM.from_pretrained(model_name)

# Example input text
text = "The quick brown [MASK] jumps over the lazy dog."

# Tokenize input text
input_ids = tokenizer.encode(text, return_tensors="pt")

# Masked Language Modeling (MLM)
outputs = model(input_ids)

# Get the predicted tokens
predicted_index = torch.argmax(outputs.logits, dim=-1)
predicted_token = tokenizer.convert_ids_to_tokens(predicted_index[0])

# Print the predicted token
print("Predicted token:", predicted_token)
```

In this code:
- We import the necessary libraries, including **torch** and **transformers**.
- We load the pre-trained BERT model and tokenizer using the **BertTokenizer** and **BertForMaskedLM** classes from the **transformers** library.

- We define an example input text with a masked token **[MASK]**.

- We tokenize the input text using the tokenizer.

- We pass the tokenized input to the pre-trained BERT model to perform Masked Language Modeling (MLM), which predicts the masked token.

- We extract the index of the predicted token with the highest probability and convert it back to the corresponding token using the tokenizer.

- Finally, we print the predicted token.

This code demonstrates how to perform Masked Language Modeling using a pre-trained BERT model. You can adjust the input text and model to perform MLM with different masked tokens and pre-trained models.

2. **Next Sentence Prediction (NSP):**
    - NSP is a pre-training objective used specifically in models like BERT.

    - In NSP, the model is trained to predict whether a given pair of sentences appear consecutively in the original corpus or are sampled randomly from the corpus.

    - During pre-training, each training example consists of two consecutive sentences: a positive example where the two sentences are consecutive in the original corpus, and a negative example where the two sentences are randomly sampled from the corpus.

    - The model is trained to predict whether the second sentence follows the first sentence (label 1) or not (label 0).

    - NSP helps the model learn relationships between sentences and capture discourse-level information.

Next Sentence Prediction (NSP) is a pre-training objective used in models like BERT. Here's a Python code example demonstrating how to perform Next Sentence Prediction using a pre-trained BERT model and the Hugging Face transformers library:

```python
from transformers import BertTokenizer, BertForNextSentencePrediction
import torch

# Load pre-trained BERT model and tokenizer
model_name = "bert-base-uncased"
tokenizer = BertTokenizer.from_pretrained(model_name)
model = BertForNextSentencePrediction.from_pretrained(model_name)

# Example input sentences
sentence1 = "The quick brown fox jumps over the lazy dog."
sentence2 = "He is very energetic."

# Tokenize input sentences
inputs = tokenizer(sentence1, sentence2, return_tensors="pt", padding=True, truncation=True)

# Next Sentence Prediction (NSP)
outputs = model(**inputs)

# Get the predicted next sentence label
predicted_label = torch.argmax(outputs.logits, dim=1).item()

# Print the predicted next sentence label
print("Predicted next sentence label:", predicted_label)
```

In this code:

- We import the necessary libraries, including **torch** and **transformers**.

- We load the pre-trained BERT model and tokenizer using the **BertTokenizer** and **BertForNextSentencePrediction** classes from the **transformers** library.

- We define example input sentences.

- We tokenize the input sentences using the tokenizer.

- We pass the tokenized inputs to the pre-trained BERT model to perform Next Sentence Prediction (NSP), which predicts whether the second sentence follows the first sentence.

- We extract the index of the predicted next sentence label and print it out.

This code demonstrates how to perform Next Sentence Prediction using a pre-trained BERT model. You can adjust the input sentences and model to perform NSP with different pairs of sentences and pre-trained models.

Here's a high-level overview of how you might implement these pre-training objectives using the Hugging Face **transformers** library:

```python
from transformers import BertTokenizer, BertForPreTraining
import torch

# Load pre-trained BERT model and tokenizer
model_name = "bert-base-uncased"
tokenizer = BertTokenizer.from_pretrained(model_name)
model = BertForPreTraining.from_pretrained(model_name)

# Example input text
text = "The quick brown fox jumps over the lazy dog."

# Tokenize input text
input_ids = tokenizer.encode(text, return_tensors="pt")

# Masked Language Modeling (MLM)
labels = input_ids.clone()
masked_indices = torch.rand(input_ids.shape) < 0.15  # Mask 15% of tokens
masked_indices &= input_ids != tokenizer.cls_token_id  # Don't mask [CLS] token
masked_indices &= input_ids != tokenizer.sep_token_id  # Don't mask [SEP] token
input_ids[masked_indices] = tokenizer.mask_token_id
outputs = model(input_ids=input_ids, labels=labels)

# Next Sentence Prediction (NSP)
next_sentence_labels = torch.tensor([1])  # Next sentence label
outputs = model(input_ids=input_ids, next_sentence_label=next_sentence_labels)
```

In this example:

- We import the necessary libraries, including **torch** and **transformers**.

- We load the pre-trained BERT model and tokenizer using the **BertTokenizer** and **BertForPreTraining** classes from the **transformers** library.

- We define an example input text.

- We tokenize the input text using the tokenizer.

- For MLM, we randomly mask 15% of the tokens in the input sequence, excluding special tokens like **[CLS]** and **[SEP]**, and replace them with the **[MASK]** token. We then pass the masked input to the model along with the original input to predict the original tokens.

- For NSP, we define the next sentence label (1 for consecutive sentences, 0 for randomly sampled sentences) and pass the input to the model along with the next sentence label to predict whether the second sentence follows the first sentence.

You can adjust the percentage of tokens to mask for MLM and the labels for NSP based on your specific use case.

Training Procedure in LLM

The training procedure for Large Language Models (LLMs) like BERT, GPT, or T5 involves several steps, including data pre-processing, model configuration, hyperparameter tuning, and optimization. Below is a general outline of the training procedure for LLMs:

1. **Data Collection and Pre-processing**:

Data collection and pre-processing are crucial steps in training Large Language Models (LLMs) like BERT, GPT, or T5. These steps involve gathering a large corpus of text data from diverse sources and preparing it for training. Here's a detailed description of data collection and pre-processing for LLMs:

1. **Data Collection**:

    - **Source Selection**: Determine the sources from which to collect text data. These sources may include books, articles, websites, social media platforms, academic papers, forums, blogs, and other publicly available text repositories.

    - **Data Rights and Permissions**: Ensure compliance with data rights and permissions, especially when collecting data from copyrighted sources or user-generated content.

    - **Data Diversity**: Aim for a diverse and representative dataset that covers a wide range of topics, genres, languages, and writing styles. Diversity helps improve the generalization and robustness of the trained LLM.

    - **Data Volume**: Collect a large amount of text data to train LLMs effectively. Large-scale datasets containing millions or even billions of text samples are common for training state-of-the-art LLMs.

2. **Data Pre-processing**:

    - **Text Cleaning**: Clean the collected text data to remove noise, inconsistencies, and irrelevant information. Common cleaning steps include:
        - Removing HTML tags, URLs, and special characters.
        - Lowercasing all text to ensure uniformity.
        - Removing punctuation marks, digits, and non-alphanumeric characters.

    - **Tokenization**: Tokenize the cleaned text into individual tokens, such as words or subwords. Tokenization breaks the text into smaller units that the model can process. Common tokenization techniques include word-based tokenization, subword tokenization (e.g., Byte-Pair Encoding), and character-level tokenization.

- **Vocabulary Construction**: Build a vocabulary of tokens from the preprocessed text data. The vocabulary contains a mapping of tokens to numerical indices that the model can understand. It typically includes the most frequent tokens in the dataset and special tokens like **[CLS], [SEP], [MASK], and [UNK]**.

- **Sequence Length Normalization**: Normalize the length of input sequences by padding or truncating them to a fixed length. Most LLMs accept fixed-length input sequences, so sequences longer than the maximum allowed length need to be truncated, and shorter sequences need to be padded with special tokens.

- **Labeling (Optional)**: If the data is labeled for supervised learning tasks like text classification, named entity recognition, or sentiment analysis, assign appropriate labels to each sample in the dataset.

3. **Dataset Splitting**:

    - **Training Set**: Divide the pre-processed data into a training set, which is used to train the LLM.

    - **Validation Set**: Set aside a portion of the data as a validation set to monitor the model's performance during training and tune hyperparameters.

    - **Test Set**: Reserve another portion of the data as a test set to evaluate the trained model's performance on unseen data.

By meticulously collecting and pre-processing data, you can create high-quality datasets that facilitate effective training of Large Language Models for various natural language processing tasks. These datasets play a critical role in determining the performance and generalization capabilities of the trained LLMs.

2. **Model Selection and Configuration**:
   Model selection and configuration are critical steps in training Large Language Models (LLMs) like BERT, GPT, or T5. Here's a detailed description of model selection and configuration for LLMs:

   1. **Model Selection**:

      - **Choose Architecture**: Select an appropriate LLM architecture based on the requirements of your task and computational resources available. Common LLM architectures include:
        o Transformer-based models like BERT, GPT, RoBERTa, and T5.
        o Recurrent Neural Network (RNN) based models like LSTM and GRU.
        o Convolutional Neural Network (CNN) based models for text classification and sentiment analysis.
      - **Consider Pre-trained Models**: Consider using pre-trained LLMs that have been pre-trained on large text corpora. Pre-trained models often provide strong performance across a wide range of natural language processing tasks and can be fine-tuned on task-specific data.

   2. **Model Configuration**:

      - **Architecture Parameters**: Configure the architecture parameters of the selected LLM based on the task requirements and computational constraints. Common architecture parameters include:
        o Number of layers: Determine the depth of the model by specifying the number of layers in the encoder and decoder stacks.
        o Hidden size: Set the dimensionality of the hidden states and embedding vectors.
        o Attention heads: Specify the number of attention heads in multi-head attention mechanisms.

- **Sequence Length**: Define the maximum sequence length that the model can process. This parameter determines the input size and influences memory requirements.

- **Vocabulary Size**: Specify the size of the vocabulary used for tokenization. The vocabulary size should be large enough to cover all tokens in the training data.

- **Initialization**: Initialize the model's parameters using appropriate initialization techniques, such as Xavier or Kaiming initialization, to ensure stable training.

- **Activation Functions**: Choose activation functions for non-linear transformations, such as ReLU, sigmoid, or tanh, based on the model's architecture and task requirements.

- **Dropout and Regularization**: Apply dropout regularization to prevent overfitting by randomly dropping units during training. Tune the dropout rate based on the complexity of the model and the amount of available training data.

- **Optimizer and Learning Rate**: Select an optimizer (e.g., Adam, SGD) and set the learning rate schedule to control the rate of parameter updates during training. Adjust the learning rate based on the model's convergence behaviour and performance on the validation set.

- **Loss Function**: Choose an appropriate loss function for the task at hand, such as cross-entropy loss for classification tasks or mean squared error for regression tasks.
- **Evaluation Metrics**: Define evaluation metrics to assess the model's performance on the validation set and monitor its progress during training. Common evaluation metrics include accuracy, precision, recall, F1-score, and perplexity.

By carefully selecting and configuring the model architecture and parameters, you can build and train LLMs that are well-suited to your specific natural language processing tasks and achieve optimal performance.

3. **Fine-tuning (Optional)**:

- Fine-tuning is a crucial step in training Large Language Models (LLMs) like BERT, GPT, or T5 for specific downstream tasks such as text classification, named entity recognition, or text generation. Here's a detailed description of the fine-tuning process for LLMs:

Pre-trained Model Selection:

- Choose a pre-trained LLM model that best matches the requirements of your downstream task. Pre-trained models are typically trained on large text corpora and are fine-tuned on task-specific data to adapt them to the target task.

- Consider factors such as the architecture (e.g., BERT, GPT, T5), pre-training objective, model size, and computational resources available.

Task-specific Data Preparation:

- Collect or annotate task-specific data relevant to your downstream task. Ensure that the data is representative of the target domain and covers the range of input variations expected during inference.

- Pre-process the data by tokenizing, padding, and encoding it into a format suitable for input to the pre-trained LLM model.

Fine-tuning Procedure:

- Initialize the pre-trained LLM model with its weights from the pre-training phase.

- Define the task-specific fine-tuning objective, loss function, and evaluation metrics appropriate for the target task.

- Prepare the training, validation, and test datasets, ensuring that they are split and formatted correctly.

- Fine-tune the model on the task-specific data by updating its parameters using gradient-based optimization algorithms such as stochastic gradient descent (SGD), Adam, or Adagrad.

- Iterate over the training dataset in mini-batches, compute gradients of the loss function with respect to the model parameters, and update the parameters using backpropagation.

- Monitor the training process by evaluating the model's performance on the validation dataset at regular intervals and adjusting hyperparameters as needed.

- Optionally, apply techniques such as learning rate scheduling, early stopping, or model checkpointing to improve training efficiency and prevent overfitting.

Evaluation and Model Selection:

- Evaluate the fine-tuned model on the held-out test dataset to assess its performance on unseen data.

- Compute evaluation metrics relevant to the target task, such as accuracy, precision, recall, F1-score, or perplexity.
- Analyse the model's predictions and errors to identify areas for improvement and potential biases.

- Compare the performance of different fine-tuned models and select the best-performing model based on the evaluation results.

Deployment and Inference:

- Deploy the fine-tuned model to production environments for inference on new data.

- Integrate the model into your application or pipeline, ensuring compatibility with input data formats and processing requirements.

- Monitor the deployed model's performance and retrain or fine-tune it periodically as needed to maintain optimal performance over time.

- By following these steps, you can effectively fine-tune pre-trained LLMs for specific downstream tasks and achieve high performance on task-specific data. Fine-tuning allows you to leverage the rich representations learned during pre-training and adapt them to your target task, reducing the need for extensive labeled data and training resources.

- **Training**:

  - Initialize the LLM model with pre-trained weights or random weights.

  - Define the training objective or loss function based on the task (e.g., cross-entropy loss for classification, negative log-likelihood for language modeling).

  - Train the model using gradient-based optimization algorithms such as stochastic gradient descent (SGD), Adam, or Adagrad.

  - Iterate over the training dataset in mini-batches, computing gradients of the loss function with respect to the model parameters, and updating the parameters using backpropagation.

  - Monitor the training process by evaluating the model's performance on a validation dataset at regular intervals and adjusting hyperparameters as needed.

- **Evaluation**:

  - Evaluate the trained model on a held-out test dataset to assess its performance on unseen data.

  - Compute evaluation metrics relevant to the task, such as accuracy, precision, recall, F1-score, or perplexity.

- Analyze the model's predictions and errors to identify areas for improvement.

4. **Hyperparameter Tuning and Optimization**:

Hyperparameter tuning and optimization play a crucial role in training Large Language Models (LLMs) like BERT, GPT, or T5 to achieve optimal performance on downstream tasks. Here's a detailed description of hyperparameter tuning and optimization in LLMs:

Hyperparameter Selection:

Identify the hyperparameters that have a significant impact on the performance of the LLM model. Common hyperparameters include:

- Learning rate: Controls the step size during parameter updates in optimization algorithms like SGD or Adam.

- Batch size: Specifies the number of training examples processed in each optimization step.

- Dropout rate: Determines the proportion of units randomly dropped during training to prevent overfitting.

- Number of layers: Sets the depth of the model architecture, influencing its capacity to capture complex patterns.

- Hidden size: Specifies the dimensionality of hidden states and embedding vectors.

- Attention heads: Determines the number of attention heads in multi-head attention mechanisms.

- Sequence length: Defines the maximum length of input sequences accepted by the model.

- Choose an appropriate range or distribution for each hyperparameter based on prior knowledge, empirical evidence, or domain expertise.

5. **Hyperparameter Tuning Methods:**

- Grid Search: Exhaustively search through a predefined grid of hyperparameter combinations and evaluate the model's performance on a validation dataset for each combination.

- Random Search: Randomly sample hyperparameter combinations from predefined ranges or distributions and evaluate their performance on a validation dataset.

- Bayesian Optimization: Use probabilistic models to predict the performance of different hyperparameter configurations and select new configurations to evaluate based on past observations.

- Population-Based Methods: Maintain a population of hyperparameter configurations and iteratively evolve them based on their performance, inspired by evolutionary algorithms.

- Automated Hyperparameter Tuning Tools: Utilize automated machine learning (AutoML) platforms or libraries like Optuna, Hyperopt, or Ray Tune to automate the hyperparameter tuning process and efficiently explore the hyperparameter space.

Hyperparameter Optimization Procedure:

- Define an objective function that quantifies the model's performance on a validation dataset using evaluation metrics relevant to the target task (e.g., accuracy, F1-score).

- Split the training dataset into training and validation sets to facilitate hyperparameter tuning without overfitting.

- Choose a hyperparameter tuning method (e.g., grid search, random search, Bayesian optimization) and specify the search space for each hyperparameter.

- Run the hyperparameter tuning process, evaluating the model's performance for each hyperparameter configuration on the validation dataset.

- Select the hyperparameter configuration that yields the best performance on the validation dataset and use it to train the final model on the entire training dataset.
- Evaluate the final model's performance on a held-out test dataset to assess its generalization ability on unseen data.

Best Practices:

- Monitor the hyperparameter tuning process and adjust the search space, search strategy, or optimization algorithm based on the observed performance trends.

- Regularize the hyperparameter search to prevent overfitting to the validation dataset by using techniques like early stopping, cross-validation, or Bayesian optimization with warm-starts.

- Balance the trade-off between computational resources and search efficiency by selecting an appropriate hyperparameter tuning method and search budget.

- Document the hyperparameter tuning process, including the search space, search strategy, and evaluation results, to facilitate reproducibility and knowledge sharing.

By carefully tuning and optimizing hyperparameters, you can maximize the performance of Large Language Models on downstream tasks and achieve state-of-the-art results with efficient resource utilization.

6. **Deployment**:

Deployment of Large Language Models (LLMs) involves integrating trained models into production environments for inference on new data. Here's a detailed description of the deployment process for LLMs:

- **Model Serialization:**
    - Serialize the trained LLM model into a format suitable for deployment. Common serialization formats include ONNX, TensorFlow SavedModel, PyTorch JIT Script, or Hugging Face Transformers save_pretrained format.
    - Serialize associated artifacts such as tokenizers, vocabulary files, and configuration files required for model inference.

- **Model Packaging:**
    - Package the serialized model and associated artifacts into a deployable unit. Depending on the deployment environment, this could be a Docker container, a Python package, or a standalone binary.
    - Include dependencies and runtime environments necessary for model inference, such as the appropriate version of Python, PyTorch or TensorFlow libraries, and any third-party dependencies.

- **API Design:**

    - Design an API (Application Programming Interface) for interacting with the deployed LLM model. The API defines the input and output formats, as well as the endpoints for making predictions.

    - Choose an appropriate API protocol, such as RESTful APIs, gRPC, or GraphQL, based on the deployment requirements and infrastructure.

- **Model Serving:**

    - Set up a model serving infrastructure to host and manage the deployed LLM model. This could be done using cloud-based services like AWS Lambda, Google Cloud Functions, or Azure Functions, or using self-hosted solutions like Flask, FastAPI, or TensorFlow Serving.

- Configure the model serving infrastructure to handle incoming requests, preprocess input data, perform model inference, and post-process output predictions.

- Ensure scalability, fault tolerance, and resource efficiency of the model serving infrastructure to handle varying workloads and traffic patterns.

- **Monitoring and Logging:**
  - Implement monitoring and logging mechanisms to track the performance, health, and usage of the deployed LLM model. Monitor metrics such as latency, throughput, error rates, and resource utilization to ensure optimal performance and reliability.
  - Integrate with logging frameworks and monitoring tools to capture and analyse logs, alerts, and metrics in real-time.

- **Security and Compliance:**
  - Implement security measures to protect the deployed LLM model from unauthorized access, data breaches, and adversarial attacks. Use authentication, authorization, encryption, and other security protocols to safeguard sensitive data and resources.
  - Ensure compliance with regulatory requirements, privacy laws, and data protection policies governing the use of sensitive information in deployed models.

- **Versioning and Rollback:**
  - Establish version control mechanisms to manage multiple versions of the deployed LLM model and track changes over time. Use versioning to rollback to previous versions in case of performance degradation or unexpected issues.

- o Implement blue-green deployment or canary deployment strategies to gradually roll out new versions of the model and minimize downtime or disruption.

- **Documentation and Training:**

  - o Document the deployment process, including setup instructions, API documentation, configuration details, and troubleshooting guides, to facilitate deployment and usage by other team members or stakeholders.

  - o Provide training and support to stakeholders, developers, and end-users on how to interact with the deployed LLM model, make predictions, and interpret results.

  - o By following these steps, you can effectively deploy Large Language Models into production environments and leverage their capabilities for real-world applications in various domains, including natural language understanding, generation, and dialogue systems.

7. Monitoring and Maintenance:

Monitoring and maintenance are essential aspects of managing deployed Large Language Models (LLMs) in production environments. Here's a detailed description of monitoring and maintenance practices for LLMs:

Performance Monitoring:

- Monitor key performance metrics of the deployed LLM, including inference latency, throughput, error rates, and resource utilization (CPU, memory, GPU).

- Use monitoring tools and frameworks to collect, analyse, and visualize performance metrics in real-time, allowing you to detect anomalies, bottlenecks, and performance degradation.

- Set up alerts and notifications to alert the operations team or developers when performance metrics exceed predefined thresholds or anomalies are detected.

Model Health Monitoring:

- Monitor the health and stability of the deployed LLM model by tracking evaluation metrics such as accuracy, precision, recall, F1-score, or perplexity.

- Periodically evaluate the model's performance on a validation dataset or through A/B testing to assess its generalization ability and identify potential drift or degradation.

- Implement model versioning and rollback mechanisms to revert to previous versions of the model in case of performance deterioration or unexpected issues.

Data Drift and Concept Drift Detection:

- Monitor for data drift and concept drift in the input data distribution to detect changes in the underlying data patterns or concepts over time.

- Use statistical methods, drift detection algorithms, and domain-specific knowledge to analyse input data distributions and identify deviations from the training data distribution.

- Adapt the deployed LLM model or retrain it with updated data to address data drift and concept drift and maintain model performance over time.

Resource Management:

- Monitor resource utilization (CPU, memory, GPU) of the infrastructure hosting the deployed LLM model to ensure optimal resource allocation and efficient utilization.

- Scale the infrastructure horizontally or vertically based on workload demands, traffic patterns, and resource constraints to handle varying workloads and maintain performance stability.

Security and Compliance:

- Monitor access logs and audit trails to track user interactions with the deployed LLM model and detect potential security threats, unauthorized access attempts, or data breaches.

- Implement security controls, encryption, access controls, and compliance measures to protect sensitive data and ensure compliance with regulatory requirements and privacy laws.

Automated Testing and Validation:

- Implement automated testing frameworks and validation pipelines to verify the correctness, robustness, and reliability of the deployed LLM model under different scenarios and edge cases.

- Conduct regular regression testing, integration testing, and end-to-end testing to validate the functionality and performance of the deployed LLM model across different environments and use cases.

Regular Maintenance and Updates:

- Perform regular maintenance activities such as software updates, security patches, and bug fixes to keep the deployed LLM model up-to-date and secure.

- Continuously monitor the development of new techniques, algorithms, and advancements in the field of natural language processing (NLP) to incorporate improvements and enhancements into the deployed model.

Documentation and Knowledge Sharing:

- Document monitoring procedures, maintenance tasks, troubleshooting steps, and best practices for managing deployed LLMs to facilitate knowledge sharing and collaboration among team members.

- Provide training and support to operations teams, developers, and stakeholders on how to effectively monitor, maintain, and troubleshoot the deployed LLM model.

By implementing comprehensive monitoring and maintenance practices, you can ensure the reliable operation, performance, and security of deployed Large Language Models in production environments and deliver high-quality services to end-users and stakeholders.

By following these steps, you can train and deploy Large Language Models effectively for various natural language processing tasks.

Fine-tuning Strategies in LLM

Fine-tuning strategies for Large Language Models (LLMs) involve techniques to adapt pre-trained models like BERT, GPT, or T5 to specific downstream tasks. Here are some fine-tuning strategies commonly used in LLMs:

Task-specific Adaptation:

- Fine-tune the pre-trained LLM on task-specific data to adapt it to the target task. This involves updating the model's parameters using gradient-based optimization algorithms on a task-specific objective function.

- Task-specific adaptation allows the LLM to learn task-specific patterns, features, and representations from labeled or annotated data, enhancing its performance on the target task.

Task-specific adaptation, often referred to as fine-tuning, involves training a pre-trained language model on task-specific data to adapt it to the target task. Here's a step-by-step guide on how to perform task-specific adaptation with Python code using the Hugging Face Transformers library:

Install Dependencies:
Install the Hugging Face Transformers library, which provides pre-trained models and tools for natural language processing tasks.

pip install transformers
Load Pre-trained Model:

- Load a pre-trained language model using the **AutoModelForSequenceClassification** class for classification tasks or the **AutoModelForSequenceClassification** class for sequence labeling tasks like named entity recognition (NER) or part-of-speech (POS) tagging.

from transformers import AutoTokenizer, AutoModelForSequenceClassification

# Load pre-trained BERT model and tokenizer
model_name = "bert-base-uncased"
tokenizer = AutoTokenizer.from_pretrained(model_name)
model = AutoModelForSequenceClassification.from_pretrained(model_name)

Prepare Task-specific Data:

- Prepare task-specific data in the required format for the target task. For sequence classification tasks, the data should consist of input texts and corresponding labels. For sequence labeling tasks, the data should consist of input texts and token-level labels.

# Example classification data
train_texts = ["Text 1", "Text 2", ...]
train_labels = [0, 1, ...] # Label indices corresponding to each input text

Tokenization and Encoding:

- Tokenize and encode the input texts using the tokenizer to convert them into input features suitable for the model.

```
# Tokenize and encode input texts
train_encodings = tokenizer(train_texts, truncation=True, padding=True)
```

Fine-tuning:

- Fine-tune the pre-trained model on the task-specific data by training it using gradient descent optimization on the task-specific objective function.

```
import torch
from torch.utils.data import Dataset, DataLoader
from transformers import AdamW

class CustomDataset(Dataset):
    def __init__(self, encodings, labels):
        self.encodings = encodings
        self.labels = labels

    def __len__(self):
        return len(self.labels)

    def __getitem__(self, idx):
        return {key: torch.tensor(val[idx]) for key, val in self.encodings.items()}, torch.tensor(self.labels[idx])

# Create DataLoader for training data
train_dataset = CustomDataset(train_encodings, train_labels)
train_loader = DataLoader(train_dataset, batch_size=32, shuffle=True)

# Define optimizer and learning rate scheduler
optimizer = AdamW(model.parameters(), lr=5e-5)
num_epochs = 3

# Fine-tune the model
for epoch in range(num_epochs):
    model.train()
    for batch in train_loader:
        optimizer.zero_grad()
```

```
input_ids = batch['input_ids'].to(device)
attention_mask = batch['attention_mask'].to(device)
labels = batch['labels'].to(device)
outputs           =           model(input_ids=input_ids,
attention_mask=attention_mask, labels=labels)
loss = outputs.loss
loss.backward()
optimizer.step()
```

Evaluation:

- Evaluate the fine-tuned model on a validation dataset to assess its performance on unseen data and adjust hyperparameters as needed.

```
# Example evaluation
model.eval()
with torch.no_grad():
    # Evaluate on validation dataset
    val_loss = 0
    for batch in val_loader:
        input_ids = batch['input_ids'].to(device)
        attention_mask = batch['attention_mask'].to(device)
        labels = batch['labels'].to(device)
        outputs           =           model(input_ids=input_ids,
attention_mask=attention_mask, labels=labels)
        val_loss += outputs.loss.item()
    avg_val_loss = val_loss / len(val_loader)
```

Inference:

- Use the fine-tuned model for inference on new data by tokenizing, encoding, and passing the input through the model to obtain predictions.

```
# Example inference
text = "New text to classify"
encoded_text = tokenizer(text, truncation=True, padding=True, return_tensors="pt")
logits = model(**encoded_text).logits
predicted_class = torch.argmax(logits, dim=1).item()
```

This Python code demonstrates how to perform task-specific adaptation (fine-tuning) of a pre-trained language model using the Hugging Face Transformers library. Make sure to adapt the code according to your specific task, dataset, and model requirements.

Transfer Learning:

- Leverage transfer learning by initializing the pre-trained LLM with weights learned during pre-training on a large corpus of text data. Fine-tune the model's parameters on a smaller task-specific dataset to transfer knowledge learned during pre-training to the target task.

- Transfer learning enables the LLM to leverage the rich representations and linguistic knowledge acquired during pre-training, reducing the need for extensive labeled data and training resources for downstream tasks.

Transfer learning in Large Language Models (LLMs) involves leveraging knowledge learned from pre-training on large text corpora and transferring it to downstream tasks with limited labeled data. Here's a step-by-step guide on how to perform transfer learning in LLMs using Python code with the Hugging Face Transformers library:

Install Dependencies:

- Install the Hugging Face Transformers library and other necessary dependencies.

pip install transformers

Load Pre-trained Model:
- Load a pre-trained LLM model using the **AutoModelForSequenceClassification** class for classification tasks or the **AutoModelForTokenClassification** class for sequence labeling tasks like named entity recognition (NER) or part-of-speech (POS) tagging.

from transformers import AutoTokenizer, AutoModelForSequenceClassification

```
# Load pre-trained BERT model and tokenizer
model_name = "bert-base-uncased"
tokenizer = AutoTokenizer.from_pretrained(model_name)
model = AutoModelForSequenceClassification.from_pretrained(model_name)
```

Prepare Task-specific Data:

- Prepare task-specific data in the required format for the target task. For sequence classification tasks, the data should consist of input texts and corresponding labels. For sequence labeling tasks, the data should consist of input texts and token-level labels.

```
# Example classification data
train_texts = ["Text 1", "Text 2", ...]
train_labels = [0, 1, ...]  # Label indices corresponding to each input text
```

Tokenization and Encoding:
- Tokenize and encode the input texts using the tokenizer to convert them into input features suitable for the model.

```
# Tokenize and encode input texts
train_encodings = tokenizer(train_texts, truncation=True, padding=True)
```

Fine-tuning:

- Fine-tune the pre-trained model on the task-specific data by training it using gradient descent optimization on the task-specific objective function.

```
import torch
from torch.utils.data import Dataset, DataLoader
from transformers import AdamW

class CustomDataset(Dataset):
    def __init__(self, encodings, labels):
        self.encodings = encodings
        self.labels = labels
```

```python
    def __len__(self):
        return len(self.labels)

    def __getitem__(self, idx):
        return {key: torch.tensor(val[idx]) for key, val in self.encodings.items()}, torch.tensor(self.labels[idx])

# Create DataLoader for training data
train_dataset = CustomDataset(train_encodings, train_labels)
train_loader = DataLoader(train_dataset, batch_size=32, shuffle=True)

# Define optimizer and learning rate scheduler
optimizer = AdamW(model.parameters(), lr=5e-5)
num_epochs = 3

# Fine-tune the model
for epoch in range(num_epochs):
    model.train()
    for batch in train_loader:
        optimizer.zero_grad()
        input_ids = batch['input_ids'].to(device)
        attention_mask = batch['attention_mask'].to(device)
        labels = batch['labels'].to(device)
        outputs = model(input_ids=input_ids, attention_mask=attention_mask, labels=labels)
        loss = outputs.loss
        loss.backward()
        optimizer.step()
```

Evaluation:

- Evaluate the fine-tuned model on a validation dataset to assess its performance on unseen data and adjust hyperparameters as needed.

```python
# Example evaluation
model.eval()
with torch.no_grad():
    # Evaluate on validation dataset
    val_loss = 0
    for batch in val_loader:
        input_ids = batch['input_ids'].to(device)
```

```
    attention_mask = batch['attention_mask'].to(device)
    labels = batch['labels'].to(device)
    outputs = model(input_ids=input_ids, attention_mask=attention_mask, labels=labels)
    val_loss += outputs.loss.item()
  avg_val_loss = val_loss / len(val_loader)
```

Inference:

- Use the fine-tuned model for inference on new data by tokenizing, encoding, and passing the input through the model to obtain predictions.

```
# Example inference
text = "New text to classify"
encoded_text = tokenizer(text, truncation=True, padding=True, return_tensors="pt")
logits = model(**encoded_text).logits
predicted_class = torch.argmax(logits, dim=1).item()
```

This Python code demonstrates how to perform transfer learning in Large Language Models (LLMs) using the Hugging Face Transformers library. Make sure to adapt the code according to your specific task, dataset, and model requirements.

Multi-task Learning:

- Train the LLM on multiple related tasks simultaneously by jointly optimizing a shared model for multiple objective functions. This allows the model to learn shared representations across tasks and benefit from the synergy between tasks.

- Multi-task learning can improve the generalization ability, robustness, and performance of the LLM by leveraging complementary information from multiple tasks.

Multi-task learning involves training a single model to perform multiple tasks simultaneously, leveraging shared representations across tasks to improve performance. Below is an example Python code for multi-task learning using the Hugging Face Transformers library:

```python
import torch
from torch.utils.data import DataLoader
from transformers import AutoTokenizer, AutoModelForSequenceClassification, AdamW
from datasets import load_dataset

# Load pre-trained model and tokenizer
model_name = "bert-base-uncased"
tokenizer = AutoTokenizer.from_pretrained(model_name)
model = AutoModelForSequenceClassification.from_pretrained(model_name)

# Define tasks and corresponding datasets
tasks = ["task1", "task2"]  # Example tasks
datasets = {}

# Load or prepare datasets for each task (replace with your own datasets)
for task in tasks:
    datasets[task] = load_dataset(task)

# Define training parameters
optimizer = AdamW(model.parameters(), lr=5e-5)
num_epochs = 3
batch_size = 32

# Define DataLoader for each task
dataloaders = {}
for task, dataset in datasets.items():
    dataloaders[task] = DataLoader(dataset['train'], batch_size=batch_size, shuffle=True)

# Define loss functions for each task
loss_functions = {}

# Fine-tune the model on multiple tasks
for epoch in range(num_epochs):
    model.train()
    for task, dataloader in dataloaders.items():
        for batch in dataloader:
            optimizer.zero_grad()
            input_ids = batch['input_ids'].to(device)
            attention_mask = batch['attention_mask'].to(device)
```

```
        labels = batch['labels'].to(device)
        outputs = model(input_ids=input_ids,
attention_mask=attention_mask, labels=labels)
        loss = outputs.loss
        loss.backward()
        optimizer.step()
```

In this code:
- We first load a pre-trained model (e.g., BERT) and tokenizer.
- We define multiple tasks and corresponding datasets. You should replace the example tasks and datasets with your own.
- For each task, we define a DataLoader to iterate through the dataset during training.
- We define loss functions for each task. You should replace the example loss functions with appropriate ones for your tasks.
- We train the model on multiple tasks simultaneously by iterating through each task's DataLoader and updating the model parameters based on the loss calculated for each task.

This code demonstrates a basic multi-task learning setup using the Hugging Face Transformers library. Make sure to adapt it to your specific tasks, datasets, and model requirements.

Gradual Unfreezing:

- Gradually unfreeze and fine-tune different layers or blocks of the pre-trained LLM in a staged manner. Start by fine-tuning only the top layers while keeping lower layers frozen, and gradually unfreeze lower layers as training progresses.
- Gradual unfreezing allows the model to adapt to task-specific features at different levels of abstraction while retaining the knowledge learned during pre-training in the lower layers.

Gradual unfreezing involves fine-tuning different layers or blocks of a pre-trained Large Language Model (LLM) in a staged manner, starting with unfreezing only the top layers and gradually unfreezing lower layers as training progresses. Here's an example Python code for gradual unfreezing using the Hugging Face Transformers library:

```python
import torch
from torch.utils.data import DataLoader
from transformers import AutoTokenizer, AutoModelForSequenceClassification, AdamW
from datasets import load_dataset

# Load pre-trained model and tokenizer
model_name = "bert-base-uncased"
tokenizer = AutoTokenizer.from_pretrained(model_name)
model = AutoModelForSequenceClassification.from_pretrained(model_name)

# Define task-specific dataset (replace with your own dataset)
dataset = load_dataset("your_dataset")

# Define training parameters
optimizer = AdamW(model.parameters(), lr=5e-5)
num_epochs = 3
batch_size = 32

# Tokenize and encode dataset
encoded_dataset = dataset.map(lambda example: tokenizer(example['text'], padding=True, truncation=True), batched=True)

# Define DataLoader
dataloader = DataLoader(encoded_dataset['train'], batch_size=batch_size, shuffle=True)

# Gradual unfreezing
for epoch in range(num_epochs):
    model.train()
    for param in model.parameters():
        param.requires_grad = False  # Freeze all parameters initially

    # Unfreeze top layers gradually
    if epoch == 0:
        for param in model.bert.encoder.layer[-1].parameters():
            param.requires_grad = True
    elif epoch == 1:
```

```
        for param in model.bert.encoder.layer[-2:].parameters():
            param.requires_grad = True
    else:
        for param in model.bert.parameters():
            param.requires_grad = True

    for batch in dataloader:
        optimizer.zero_grad()
        input_ids = batch['input_ids'].to(device)
        attention_mask = batch['attention_mask'].to(device)
        labels = batch['labels'].to(device)
        outputs = model(input_ids=input_ids, attention_mask=attention_mask, labels=labels)
        loss = outputs.loss
        loss.backward()
        optimizer.step()
```

In this code:

- We load a pre-trained model (e.g., BERT) and tokenizer.
- We define a task-specific dataset. You should replace **"your_dataset"** with the name of your dataset loaded using the **load_dataset** function.
- We tokenize and encode the dataset using the tokenizer.
- We define a DataLoader for iterating through the dataset during training.
- During training, we gradually unfreeze different layers of the model based on the current epoch. In this example, we unfreeze the last layer in the first epoch, the last two layers in the second epoch, and all layers in subsequent epochs.
- We update the model parameters based on the loss calculated for each batch using the optimizer.

This code demonstrates how to implement gradual unfreezing in a Large Language Model (LLM) using the Hugging Face Transformers library. Adjust the model architecture and fine-tuning strategy as needed for your specific task and requirements.

Adaptive Learning Rate Scheduling:

- Use adaptive learning rate scheduling techniques to dynamically adjust the learning rate during fine-tuning based on the model's convergence behaviour and performance on the validation dataset.
- Techniques such as learning rate warm-up, learning rate decay, and cyclic learning rates can help stabilize training, prevent overfitting, and improve convergence speed.

Adaptive learning rate scheduling adjusts the learning rate during training based on the model's convergence behaviour and performance on the validation dataset. Here's an example Python code for adaptive learning rate scheduling using the Hugging Face Transformers library:

```
import torch
from torch.utils.data import DataLoader
from transformers import AutoTokenizer, AutoModelForSequenceClassification, AdamW, get_linear_schedule_with_warmup
from datasets import load_dataset

# Load pre-trained model and tokenizer
model_name = "bert-base-uncased"
tokenizer = AutoTokenizer.from_pretrained(model_name)
model = AutoModelForSequenceClassification.from_pretrained(model_name)

# Define task-specific dataset (replace with your own dataset)
dataset = load_dataset("your_dataset")

# Define training parameters
optimizer = AdamW(model.parameters(), lr=5e-5)
num_epochs = 3
batch_size = 32
total_steps = len(dataset['train']) * num_epochs

# Tokenize and encode dataset
encoded_dataset = dataset.map(lambda example: tokenizer(example['text'], padding=True, truncation=True), batched=True)

# Define DataLoader
```

```
dataloader       =       DataLoader(encoded_dataset['train'],
batch_size=batch_size, shuffle=True)

# Learning rate scheduling
scheduler    =    get_linear_schedule_with_warmup(optimizer,
num_warmup_steps=0, num_training_steps=total_steps)

# Training loop with adaptive learning rate scheduling
for epoch in range(num_epochs):
    model.train()
    for batch in dataloader:
        optimizer.zero_grad()
        input_ids = batch['input_ids'].to(device)
        attention_mask = batch['attention_mask'].to(device)
        labels = batch['labels'].to(device)
        outputs       =       model(input_ids=input_ids,
attention_mask=attention_mask, labels=labels)
        loss = outputs.loss
        loss.backward()
        optimizer.step()
        scheduler.step() # Update learning rate

    # Evaluation
    model.eval()
    with torch.no_grad():
        for val_batch in val_dataloader:
            val_input_ids = val_batch['input_ids'].to(device)
            val_attention_mask                        =
val_batch['attention_mask'].to(device)
            val_labels = val_batch['labels'].to(device)
            val_outputs    =    model(input_ids=val_input_ids,
attention_mask=val_attention_mask, labels=val_labels)
            val_loss = val_outputs.loss
        # Update learning rate scheduler based on validation
loss or other metrics
        scheduler.step(val_loss.item())
```

In this code:
- We load a pre-trained model (e.g., BERT) and tokenizer.
- We define a task-specific dataset. Replace **"your_dataset"** with the name of your dataset loaded using the **load_dataset** function.

- We tokenize and encode the dataset using the tokenizer.
- We define a DataLoader for iterating through the dataset during training.
- We use the **get_linear_schedule_with_warmup** function to create a scheduler that adjusts the learning rate linearly over the course of training.
- During each training epoch, we update the learning rate scheduler after each batch using the **scheduler.step()** method.
- Optionally, we can also update the learning rate scheduler based on validation loss or other metrics during evaluation.

This code demonstrates how to implement adaptive learning rate scheduling in a Large Language Model (LLM) training loop using the Hugging Face Transformers library. Adjust the scheduler parameters and training strategy as needed for your specific task and requirements.

Data Augmentation:
- Augment the training data with synthetic examples generated using data augmentation techniques such as back-translation, paraphrasing, or text perturbation.
- Data augmentation helps increase the diversity and robustness of the training data, improving the generalization ability and performance of the fine-tuned LLM on unseen data.

Data augmentation is a technique used to increase the diversity and size of the training dataset by applying transformations to the existing data. Here's an example Python code for data augmentation in Large Language Models (LLMs) using the Hugging Face Transformers library:

```
import torch
from torch.utils.data import DataLoader
from transformers import AutoTokenizer, AutoModelForSequenceClassification, AdamW
from datasets import load_dataset
import random

# Load pre-trained model and tokenizer
model_name = "bert-base-uncased"
```

```python
tokenizer = AutoTokenizer.from_pretrained(model_name)
model = AutoModelForSequenceClassification.from_pretrained(model_name)

# Define task-specific dataset (replace with your own dataset)
dataset = load_dataset("your_dataset")

# Define data augmentation functions
def random_swap(sentence, n=5):
    words = sentence.split()
    for _ in range(n):
        idx1, idx2 = random.sample(range(len(words)), 2)
        words[idx1], words[idx2] = words[idx2], words[idx1]
    return ' '.join(words)

def random_insert(sentence, n=3):
    words = sentence.split()
    for _ in range(n):
        idx = random.randint(0, len(words)-1)
        words.insert(idx, 'random_word')
    return ' '.join(words)

# Apply data augmentation
augmented_dataset = []
for example in dataset:
    text = example['text']
    augmented_text1 = random_swap(text)
    augmented_text2 = random_insert(text)
    augmented_dataset.append({'text': augmented_text1})
    augmented_dataset.append({'text': augmented_text2})

# Tokenize and encode dataset
encoded_dataset = tokenizer(augmented_dataset, padding=True, truncation=True)

# Define DataLoader
dataloader = DataLoader(encoded_dataset, batch_size=32, shuffle=True)

# Define training parameters
optimizer = AdamW(model.parameters(), lr=5e-5)
num_epochs = 3

# Training loop
```

```
for epoch in range(num_epochs):
  model.train()
  for batch in dataloader:
    optimizer.zero_grad()
    input_ids = batch['input_ids'].to(device)
    attention_mask = batch['attention_mask'].to(device)
    labels = batch['labels'].to(device)
    outputs = model(input_ids=input_ids, attention_mask=attention_mask, labels=labels)
    loss = outputs.loss
    loss.backward()
    optimizer.step()
```

In this code:

- We load a pre-trained model and tokenizer.
- We define a task-specific dataset. Replace **"your_dataset"** with the name of your dataset loaded using the **load_dataset** function.
- We define data augmentation functions (**random_swap** and **random_insert**) to perform random word swapping and random word insertion, respectively.
- We apply data augmentation to each example in the dataset, generating multiple augmented examples.
- We tokenize and encode the augmented dataset using the tokenizer.
- We define a DataLoader for iterating through the dataset during training.
- We define training parameters, such as the optimizer and number of epochs.
- We train the model using the augmented dataset.

This code demonstrates how to perform data augmentation in LLM training using the Hugging Face Transformers library. Adjust the data augmentation functions and parameters according to your specific task and requirements.

Regularization Techniques:

- Apply regularization techniques such as dropout, weight decay, or layer normalization to prevent overfitting during fine-tuning and improve the generalization ability of the LLM.

- Regularization helps mitigate the risk of overfitting to the training data and enhances the model's ability to generalize to new, unseen examples.

Regularization techniques are used to prevent overfitting during training by adding constraints on the model parameters. Here's an example Python code for applying regularization techniques in Large Language Models (LLMs) using the Hugging Face Transformers library:

```
import torch
from torch.utils.data import DataLoader
from transformers import AutoTokenizer, AutoModelForSequenceClassification, AdamW
from datasets import load_dataset
from torch.nn import CrossEntropyLoss
import torch.nn.functional as F

# Load pre-trained model and tokenizer
model_name = "bert-base-uncased"
tokenizer = AutoTokenizer.from_pretrained(model_name)
model = AutoModelForSequenceClassification.from_pretrained(model_name)

# Define task-specific dataset (replace with your own dataset)
dataset = load_dataset("your_dataset")

# Tokenize and encode dataset
encoded_dataset = dataset.map(lambda example: tokenizer(example['text'], padding=True, truncation=True), batched=True)

# Define DataLoader
dataloader = DataLoader(encoded_dataset['train'], batch_size=32, shuffle=True)

# Define training parameters
optimizer = AdamW(model.parameters(), lr=5e-5)
num_epochs = 3

# Define regularization parameters
weight_decay = 0.01
dropout_prob = 0.1
```

```python
# Training loop with regularization
for epoch in range(num_epochs):
    model.train()
    for batch in dataloader:
        optimizer.zero_grad()
        input_ids = batch['input_ids'].to(device)
        attention_mask = batch['attention_mask'].to(device)
        labels = batch['labels'].to(device)
        outputs = model(input_ids=input_ids, attention_mask=attention_mask, labels=labels)
        logits = outputs.logits
        loss = outputs.loss

        # L2 weight decay regularization
        l2_loss = sum(torch.sum(param ** 2) for param in model.parameters())
        loss += weight_decay * l2_loss

        # Dropout regularization
        dropout_loss = sum(torch.sum(F.dropout(param, p=dropout_prob)) for param in model.parameters())
        loss += dropout_loss

        loss.backward()
        optimizer.step()
```

In this code:
- We load a pre-trained model and tokenizer.
- We define a task-specific dataset. Replace **"your_dataset"** with the name of your dataset loaded using the **load_dataset** function.
- We tokenize and encode the dataset using the tokenizer.
- We define a DataLoader for iterating through the dataset during training.
- We define training parameters, such as the optimizer and number of epochs.
- We define regularization parameters, such as weight decay and dropout probability.
- During each training iteration, we compute the regularization loss and add it to the total loss before backpropagation.
- We train the model using the regularized loss.

This code demonstrates how to apply L2 weight decay and dropout regularization techniques in LLM training using the Hugging Face Transformers library. Adjust the regularization parameters according to your specific task and requirements.

By employing fine-tuning strategies effectively, you can adapt pre-trained LLMs to specific downstream tasks, improve their performance, and leverage their capabilities for various natural language processing applications.

Chapter-10   LLama (Large Language Model Meta AI)

LLama

LLama, developed by Meta AI (formerly Facebook AI), is an advanced Large Language Model designed for various natural language processing (NLP) tasks. LLama is similar to other LLMs like GPT-3, aiming to generate human-like text based on the input it receives. It leverages deep learning, specifically the transformer architecture, to achieve high performance in text generation, summarization, translation, and more.

Key Features of Llama

1. **Transformer Architecture**: Utilizes the transformer model, which is highly efficient for processing sequential data and capturing long-range dependencies in text.

2. **Pretraining on Large Datasets**: Trained on a vast amount of text data to learn language patterns, grammar, facts, and reasoning abilities.

3. **Fine-tuning Capabilities**: Can be fine-tuned on specific datasets for specialized tasks, improving performance in targeted applications.

4. **Scalability**: Designed to handle large-scale text generation tasks with ease, making it suitable for both research and commercial applications.

Getting Started with Llama

To use LLama, you can leverage libraries like Hugging Face's **transformers**, which provide a simple interface for loading and using pre-trained language models.

Installation

First, install the necessary libraries:

pip install transformers torch

Loading LLama

Here's how you can load LLama using the Hugging Face **transformers** library. Note that LLama may be available under a different name or as part of a custom implementation by Meta AI, so make sure to check the official repository or documentation for the exact model name.

from transformers import AutoModelForCausalLM, AutoTokenizer

Load the tokenizer and model

model_name = "meta-llama"

tokenizer = AutoTokenizer.from_pretrained(model_name)

model = AutoModelForCausalLM.from_pretrained(model_name)

Text Generation Example

Here's an example of generating text using LLama:

def generate_text(prompt, max_length=100, model_name="meta-llama"):

   tokenizer = AutoTokenizer.from_pretrained(model_name)

```python
model = AutoModelForCausalLM.from_pretrained(model_name)

inputs = tokenizer(prompt, return_tensors="pt")
outputs = model.generate(inputs.input_ids, max_length=max_length, num_return_sequences=1)
generated_text = tokenizer.decode(outputs[0], skip_special_tokens=True)

return generated_text


# Example prompt
prompt = "Once upon a time in a land far, far away,"
generated_text = generate_text(prompt)
print("Generated Text:\n", generated_text)
```

Fine-tuning LLama

Fine-tuning LLama on a custom dataset involves preparing your dataset and using the **Trainer** API from Hugging Face. Here's a simplified example of the process:

1. **Prepare the Dataset**

   Assume you have a text dataset stored in a file named **dataset.txt**.

```python
from datasets import load_dataset

# Load the dataset
```

```
dataset = load_dataset('text', data_files={'train': 'dataset.txt'})
```

2. **Tokenize the Dataset**

```
def tokenize_function(examples):
    return tokenizer(examples['text'], truncation=True, padding="max_length")

tokenized_datasets = dataset.map(tokenize_function, batched=True)
```

3. **Fine-tuning with Trainer**

```
from transformers import Trainer, TrainingArguments

training_args = TrainingArguments(
    output_dir="./results",
    num_train_epochs=1,
    per_device_train_batch_size=4,
    save_steps=10_000,
    save_total_limit=2,
)

trainer = Trainer(
    model=model,
    args=training_args,
    train_dataset=tokenized_datasets['train'],
)

# Start training
```

trainer.train()

Summary

LLama, developed by Meta AI, is a versatile and powerful Large Language Model that excels in various NLP tasks. Leveraging the transformer architecture, LLama can be used for text generation, summarization, and more. By utilizing libraries like Hugging Face's **transformers**, users can easily load, generate text, and fine-tune LLama on custom datasets. This makes LLama a valuable tool for both research and practical applications in the field of natural language processing.

Creating a chatbot using the LLama model

Creating a chatbot using the LLama model involves a few steps. We'll use the Hugging Face **transformers** library to leverage LLama for natural language understanding and generation. Here's a step-by-step guide to creating a simple chatbot in Python:

Step 1: Install Necessary Libraries

Ensure you have the required libraries installed:

pip install transformers torch

Step 2: Load the LLama Model

We'll load the LLama model and tokenizer. For the sake of this example, we'll assume the model is available under the name **meta-llama**. You may need to adjust the model name based on the actual model you are using.

```
from transformers import AutoModelForCausalLM, AutoTokenizer

# Load the tokenizer and model
model_name = "meta-llama"
tokenizer = AutoTokenizer.from_pretrained(model_name)
model = AutoModelForCausalLM.from_pretrained(model_name)
```

Step 3: Define the Chatbot Function

We'll create a function that takes user input, generates a response using LLama, and prints the output. The function will maintain a conversation context by appending each user input and model response.

```
def generate_response(prompt, model, tokenizer, max_length=100):
    inputs = tokenizer(prompt, return_tensors="pt")
    outputs = model.generate(inputs.input_ids, max_length=max_length, num_return_sequences=1, pad_token_id=tokenizer.eos_token_id)
    response = tokenizer.decode(outputs[0], skip_special_tokens=True)

    return response


def chat_with_llama():
    print("Start chatting with the LLama-based chatbot (type 'exit' to stop)!")

    conversation_history = ""
```

```
    while True:
        user_input = input("You: ")
        if user_input.lower() == 'exit':
            break

        conversation_history += f"You: {user_input}\n"
        prompt = conversation_history

        response = generate_response(prompt, model, tokenizer)
        conversation_history += f"Bot: {response}\n"

        print(f"Bot: {response}")

# Start the chatbot
chat_with_llama()
```

Explanation

1. **Model Loading**:

- We load the tokenizer and model using **AutoTokenizer** and **AutoModelForCausalLM** from the **transformers** library.

2. **Response Generation**:

- The **generate_response** function takes a **prompt**, which is the current conversation history, and generates a response using the LLama model. The **max_length** parameter controls the maximum length of the generated response.

3. **Chat Function**:

- The **chat_with_llama** function handles the conversation loop. It appends each user input to the conversation history and generates responses based on the accumulated conversation.

4. **Running the Chatbot**:

- The chatbot runs in an infinite loop until the user types 'exit'. Each user input is appended to the conversation history, and the model generates a context-aware response.

Step 4: Run the Chatbot

Simply run the script, and start interacting with your LLama-based chatbot:

python chatbot.py

This simple implementation maintains the conversation context by appending each user input and model response to the conversation history. For more advanced features like handling multi-turn conversations more effectively, adding personality traits, or integrating with web applications, additional logic and possibly a more sophisticated state management approach would be required.

Note

Ensure you have the appropriate model checkpoint from Meta AI or Hugging Face, and update the **model_name** variable accordingly. The above example assumes the model is accessible through the **transformers** library. If LLama is not directly available, you might need to follow specific instructions from Meta AI or use a different model from Hugging Face's repository.

Natural Language Understanding using LLAMA

To perform Natural Language Understanding (NLU) tasks using LLama, we'll utilize its capabilities for text classification. We'll fine-tune LLama on a specific dataset for a classification task, such as sentiment analysis or topic classification. Here's a step-by-step guide with a code example for text classification using LLama:

Step 1: Install Necessary Libraries

Ensure you have the required libraries installed:

pip install transformers torch datasets

Step 2: Load the LLama Model

We'll load the LLama model and tokenizer for text classification. You may need to adjust the model name based on the specific LLama variant you intend to use.

```python
from transformers import AutoModelForSequenceClassification, AutoTokenizer

# Load the tokenizer and model
model_name = "meta-llama"
tokenizer = AutoTokenizer.from_pretrained(model_name)
model = AutoModelForSequenceClassification.from_pretrained(model_name)
```

Step 3: Fine-tune LLama on a Dataset

For fine-tuning LLama, you'll need a labeled dataset suitable for the classification task. You can use datasets like IMDb for sentiment analysis or AG News for topic classification. Here's a simplified example using the IMDb dataset for sentiment analysis:

```python
from datasets import load_dataset
from transformers import Trainer, TrainingArguments

# Load the IMDb dataset
dataset = load_dataset("imdb")

# Tokenize the dataset
def tokenize(batch):
    return tokenizer(batch["text"], padding=True, truncation=True)

tokenized_dataset = dataset.map(tokenize, batched=True)

# Define training arguments
training_args = TrainingArguments(
    per_device_train_batch_size=4,
    num_train_epochs=3,
    logging_dir='./logs',
)

# Define the Trainer
```

```
trainer = Trainer(
    model=model,
    args=training_args,
    train_dataset=tokenized_dataset["train"],
)

# Fine-tune the model
trainer.train()
```

Step 4: Perform Natural Language Understanding

Once the model is fine-tuned, you can use it for natural language understanding tasks, such as sentiment analysis or topic classification, by feeding it input text and obtaining predictions.

```
def predict_sentiment(text):
    inputs = tokenizer(text, return_tensors="pt")
    outputs = model(**inputs)
    predicted_label = torch.argmax(outputs.logits)
    return "positive" if predicted_label == 1 else "negative"

# Example usage
text = "This movie was great, I loved it!"
print("Sentiment:", predict_sentiment(text))
```

Explanation

1. **Model Loading**: We load the LLama model and tokenizer for sequence classification tasks using AutoModelForSequenceClassification and AutoTokenizer from the transformers library.

2. **Fine-tuning**: We fine-tune LLama on a labeled dataset using the Trainer API from the transformers library. In this example, we use the IMDb dataset for sentiment analysis.

3. **Prediction**: After fine-tuning, we can use the model to perform sentiment analysis on new input text by obtaining predictions from the model's outputs.

Note
- Ensure you have the appropriate model checkpoint from Meta AI or Hugging Face, and update the **model_name** variable accordingly.
- Fine-tuning LLama on a specific dataset may require adjustments to the training hyperparameters and data preprocessing steps based on the characteristics of the dataset and the task at hand.
- LLama's performance on NLU tasks may vary depending on the quality and size of the training data, the fine-tuning procedure, and the specific task requirements.

Comparing LLama with other Large Language Models (LLMs)

Comparing LLama with other Large Language Models (LLMs) like GPT-3, BERT, and T5 involves examining various factors such as model architecture, capabilities, performance on different tasks, and availability of pre-trained models. Let's break down the comparison across these dimensions:

1. Model Architecture:

- **LLama**: LLama likely utilizes a transformer-based architecture, similar to other LLMs, which consists of multi-head self-attention mechanisms and feed-forward neural networks.

- **GPT-3**: GPT-3 (Generative Pre-trained Transformer 3) employs a transformer-based architecture optimized for autoregressive text generation tasks.

- **BERT**: BERT (Bidirectional Encoder Representations from Transformers) utilizes a transformer-based architecture with bidirectional attention mechanisms, pre-trained on masked language modeling and next sentence prediction tasks.

- **T5**: T5 (Text-to-Text Transfer Transformer) introduces a unified text-to-text framework for various NLP tasks, where every task is formulated as a text-to-text transformation.

2. Pre-trained Models:

- **LLama**: The availability and variety of LLama's pre-trained models may vary. Meta AI may provide pre-trained LLama models for specific tasks or release them through the Hugging Face model hub.

- **GPT-3**: OpenAI provides pre-trained versions of GPT-3 through their API, ranging from small to large sizes (e.g., 125M to 175B parameters).

- **BERT**: Pre-trained BERT models, including base and large variants, are available through the Hugging Face model hub and the original Google Research repository.

- **T5**: Similar to BERT, pre-trained T5 models are available through the Hugging Face model hub and other repositories.

3. Capabilities:

- **LLama**: LLama is designed for various NLP tasks, including text generation, summarization, translation, and possibly others depending on its fine-tuning and task-specific adaptations.

- **GPT-3**: GPT-3 excels in text generation tasks and demonstrates strong performance on a wide range of language understanding tasks.

- **BERT**: BERT is well-suited for tasks like sentence classification, sentence-pair classification, and token-level tasks such as named entity recognition (NER) and part-of-speech tagging (POS).

- **T5**: T5's text-to-text framework allows it to handle diverse NLP tasks, including translation, summarization, question answering, and text classification, by framing each task as a text-to-text transformation.

4. Performance:

- Performance comparisons across LLMs depend on the specific task and dataset being evaluated. Evaluating LLama's performance against other LLMs would require benchmarking on standardized datasets and tasks.

- GPT-3, BERT, and T5 have been extensively benchmarked on various NLP tasks, providing insights into their relative strengths and weaknesses.

Conclusion:

LLama's comparison with other LLMs involves assessing its architecture, pre-trained models, capabilities, and performance on specific NLP tasks. While LLama's details may vary compared to well-established LLMs like GPT-3, BERT, and T5, understanding these factors can help gauge its potential effectiveness in different applications and contexts. Further research and experimentation are needed to provide a comprehensive comparison across these models.

Chapter-11 Prompt Engineering

Prompt Engineering

Definition and Importance

Prompt engineering is the practice of designing and refining the inputs (prompts) given to generative AI models to elicit the desired outputs. This involves crafting specific phrases, questions, or instructions that guide the model's response. The quality and structure of the prompt play a crucial role in the effectiveness and accuracy of the generated content.

Importance:
- **Control and Precision:** Well-designed prompts can significantly improve the relevance and accuracy of AI-generated outputs.

- **Efficiency:** Efficient prompt engineering reduces the need for extensive post-processing and editing of generated content.

- **Accessibility:** Enables users, including those with limited technical expertise, to leverage the full potential of generative AI tools.
Basic Concepts and Terminology

- **Prompt:** The input or query given to a generative AI model to produce an output. Example: "Write a short story about a heroic dog."

- **Output:** The content generated by the AI in response to the prompt. Example: "Once upon a time, there was a brave dog named Rex who saved a family from a burning house."

- **Context:** The surrounding text or information provided to the model to help generate relevant outputs. This can include previous interactions or additional data.

- **Parameters:** Variables that can be adjusted to modify the behavior and performance of the AI model. Example: temperature, max tokens, etc.

- **Modifiers:** Specific instructions or keywords added to the prompt to influence the style, tone, or type of response. Example: "in a formal tone," "using technical language."

The Role of Prompts in Generative AI

Prompts serve as the primary mechanism for interacting with generative AI models. They determine the scope, style, and specificity of the generated content. The effectiveness of a prompt can be influenced by several factors:

- **Clarity and Specificity:** Clear and specific prompts are more likely to yield precise and relevant outputs.

- **Contextual Information:** Providing sufficient context helps the model understand the desired outcome better.

- **Iterative Refinement:** Continuously refining prompts based on the outputs received can enhance the quality of the responses.

Types of Prompts

1. **Simple Prompts:** Basic instructions or queries without additional context or modifiers. Example: "Tell me a joke."

2. **Complex Prompts:** Detailed instructions that include context, constraints, or multiple components. Example: "Write a motivational speech for a graduation ceremony, focusing on overcoming challenges and embracing the future."

3. **Sequential Prompts:** A series of prompts used to guide the model through a multi-step task or conversation. Example: First prompt: "Describe a futuristic city." Follow-up prompt: "Now, describe the technology used in that city."

Designing Effective Prompts

To design effective prompts, consider the following principles:

- **Understand the Model's Capabilities:** Familiarize yourself with the strengths and limitations of the AI model you're working with.

- **Be Specific:** Use clear and precise language to reduce ambiguity. Specific prompts tend to produce more accurate and relevant outputs.

- **Provide Context:** Include relevant background information or previous interactions to help the model generate more coherent responses.

- **Experiment and Iterate:** Test different prompts and refine them based on the results. Iterative refinement can significantly improve the quality of the outputs.

- **Use Modifiers Judiciously:** Apply style or tone modifiers to shape the response according to your needs. Be mindful of the impact these modifiers can have on the output.
  Examples and Case Studies

- **Customer Support:** Crafting prompts for a chatbot to handle common customer inquiries. Example: "How can I reset my password?" Refined prompt: "Explain the steps to reset my password for the online banking portal."

- **Creative Writing:** Using prompts to generate story ideas or content. Example: Initial prompt: "Write a science fiction story." Refined prompt: "Write a science fiction story set on Mars, focusing on the first human colony and their struggles with limited resources."

- **Educational Tools:** Designing prompts for interactive learning applications. Example: "Explain the Pythagorean theorem." Refined prompt: "Explain the Pythagorean theorem with an example of a right triangle with sides of 3, 4, and 5 units."

By understanding and applying the principles of prompt engineering, users can effectively harness the power of generative AI to produce high-quality, relevant, and contextually appropriate outputs. This foundational knowledge sets the stage for more advanced techniques and applications in prompt engineering.

Setting Up Your Environment

Tools and Platforms

To effectively engage in prompt engineering with generative AI, you'll need access to various tools and platforms. Here are some of the most commonly used:

1. **Generative AI Platforms:**

- **OpenAI GPT:** Offers models like GPT-3 and GPT-4 for text generation.
- **Hugging Face:** Provides a library of models, including GPT, BERT, and others.
- **Google AI:** Features models such as BERT, T5, and more through their AI Hub.
- **AI21 Labs:** Known for their language models like Jurassic-1.

2. **Integrated Development Environments (IDEs):**

- **Jupyter Notebook:** Ideal for experimenting with AI models in Python.
- **VS Code:** A versatile code editor with support for various extensions.
- **PyCharm:** Specifically designed for Python development.

3. **API Platforms:**

- **RapidAPI:** A marketplace for integrating various AI APIs.
- **Postman:** Useful for testing and managing APIs.

4. **Cloud Platforms:**

- **AWS:** Provides services like Sagemaker for machine learning.
- **Google Cloud Platform (GCP):** Offers AI and machine learning services.
- **Microsoft Azure:** Features services like Azure Machine Learning.

Installation and Configuration

Setting up your environment involves installing necessary software and configuring tools. Here are the steps for a typical setup:

1. **Python Installation:**

- Ensure you have Python installed. Download and install it from python.org.

2. **Setting Up a Virtual Environment:**

    python -m venv myenv

    source myenv/bin/activate   # On Windows use `myenv\Scripts\activate`

    Installing Required Libraries:

- Use **pip** to install libraries like **transformers**, **openai**, **numpy**, **pandas**, etc.

    pip install transformers openai numpy pandas jupyter

1. **Configuring API Access:**

- Obtain API keys from your chosen platform (e.g., OpenAI, Hugging Face).
- Store these keys securely, often in environment variables or configuration files.

2. **Setting Up Jupyter Notebook:**

- Launch Jupyter Notebook.
- Create a new notebook and start experimenting with code cells.

Working with APIs

APIs allow you to interact with generative AI models programmatically. Here's a brief guide on how to use some popular APIs:

1. **OpenAI API:**

- Install the OpenAI Python client:

```
pip install openai
```

- Example usage:

```python
import openai

openai.api_key = 'your-api-key'

response = openai.Completion.create(
    engine="text-davinci-003",
    prompt="Tell me a joke.",
    max_tokens=50
)

print(response.choices[0].text.strip())
```

Hugging Face API:

- Install the **transformers** library:

pip install transformers

- Example usage:

from transformers import pipeline

generator = pipeline('text-generation', model='gpt2')

response = generator("Tell me a joke.", max_length=50, num_return_sequences=1)

print(response[0]['generated_text'])

1. **Using Postman for API Requests:**

- Install Postman from postman.com.
- Set up a new request in Postman.
- Use the API key in the headers or query parameters.
- Test the API endpoints and inspect the responses.

Configuring Cloud Platforms

Cloud platforms offer scalable resources for more demanding AI tasks. Here's a basic setup guide:

1. **AWS Sagemaker:**

- Sign up for an AWS account.
- Navigate to Sagemaker in the AWS Management Console.
- Create a new notebook instance and configure the environment.
- Use the Sagemaker SDK to interact with models.

2. **Google Cloud AI Platform:**

- Create a Google Cloud account and set up a project.
- Enable the AI Platform services.

- Use the **gcloud** CLI to configure your environment.
- Deploy models and interact with them using the AI Platform's APIs.

3. **Azure Machine Learning:**

- Set up an Azure account and create a Machine Learning workspace.
- Use the Azure Machine Learning Studio for a visual interface.
- Configure and deploy models using the Azure SDK.

Example Setup for a Basic Project

Here's an example of setting up a basic project using OpenAI's GPT-3:

Create a Project Directory:

mkdir prompt_engineering_project

cd prompt_engineering_project

Initialize a Git Repository (Optional):

git init

Create a Virtual Environment and Install Dependencies:

python -m venv venv

source venv/bin/activate   # On Windows use `venv\Scripts\activate`

pip install openai

Create a Configuration File for API Keys:

- Create a **.env** file:

OPENAI_API_KEY=your-openai-api-key

Create a Python Script:

```
import openai

from dotenv import load_dotenv

import os

load_dotenv()

openai.api_key = os.getenv('OPENAI_API_KEY')

prompt = "Explain the theory of relativity in simple terms."

response = openai.Completion.create(
    engine="text-davinci-003",
    prompt=prompt,
    max_tokens=100
)

print(response.choices[0].text.strip())
```

Run Your Script:

python script.py

By following these steps, you'll set up a robust environment for prompt engineering with generative AI, enabling you to experiment, refine, and optimize your prompts effectively.

Basic Concepts and Techniques

Crafting Simple Prompts

The simplest form of prompt is a direct request or question. These straightforward prompts are the building blocks of more complex interactions.

Examples:

- Text: "Write a poem about the ocean."
- Image: "Generate an image of a sunset over a mountain range."

Key Points:

- **Clarity:** Ensure the prompt is clear and unambiguous.
- **Focus:** Keep the prompt focused on a single topic or task

Exploring AI Responses

Understanding how AI models generate responses is crucial for effective prompt engineering. Generative AI models use patterns learned during training to produce outputs.

Examples:

- Prompt: "What are the benefits of regular exercise?"
- Possible Response: "Regular exercise improves cardiovascular health, boosts mental well-being, and enhances physical fitness."

Key Points:

- **Patterns:** AI responses are based on patterns in the training data.
- **Diversity:** Different prompts can yield diverse responses.

Introduction to Parameters and Modifiers

Parameters and modifiers help control the output of generative AI models, allowing for customization and fine-tuning of responses.

Common Parameters:

- **Temperature:** Controls the randomness of the output. Lower values (e.g., 0.2) make the output more deterministic, while higher values (e.g., 0.8) introduce more randomness.

- **Max Tokens:** Limits the length of the generated response.

- **Top-p (Nucleus Sampling):** Controls diversity by limiting the output to a subset of possible words (e.g., top 10% most likely).

Modifiers:

- **Tone and Style:** "Write in a formal tone," "Explain as if talking to a child."

- **Contextual Information:** Adding context to the prompt for more accurate responses.

Examples:

- Temperature:

    ```
    response = openai.Completion.create(
        engine="text-davinci-003",
        prompt="Tell me a story about a dragon.",
        temperature=0.7
    )
    ```

Max Tokens:

```
response = openai.Completion.create(

  engine="text-davinci-003",

  prompt="Summarize the plot of 'Pride and Prejudice'.",

  max_tokens=50

)
```

Prompt Optimization Basics

Optimizing prompts involves refining and adjusting them to improve the relevance and quality of the AI's responses.

Techniques:

1. **Iterative Refinement:** Start with a basic prompt and iteratively improve it based on the responses.

2. **Specificity:** Add more details to the prompt to narrow down the scope of the response.

3. **Contextual Prompts:** Provide context to guide the AI in generating more accurate and relevant outputs.

4. **Testing Variations:** Test multiple variations of a prompt to find the most effective one.

Examples:

- Basic Prompt: "Describe a cat."

- Refined Prompt: "Describe a black cat with green eyes sitting on a windowsill."

Key Points:

- **Feedback Loop:** Use the outputs to inform further refinements of the prompt.

- **Goal-Oriented:** Keep the end goal in mind and tailor the prompt accordingly.

Common Pitfalls and How to Avoid Them

When crafting prompts, it's important to be aware of common pitfalls that can lead to suboptimal responses.

Pitfalls:

1. **Vagueness:** Prompts that are too vague can lead to irrelevant or generic responses.

2. **Overly Complex Prompts:** Complex prompts can confuse the model and result in incoherent outputs.

3. **Lack of Context:** Omitting necessary context can make it difficult for the model to generate accurate responses.

4. **Bias in Prompts:** Unintentionally embedding biases in prompts can lead to biased outputs.

Avoidance Strategies:

- **Clarity:** Ensure prompts are clear and specific.

- **Simplicity:** Break down complex prompts into simpler parts.

- **Context:** Provide adequate context to guide the AI.

- **Bias Check:** Review prompts for potential biases and rephrase them if necessary.

Examples:

- Vague Prompt: "What happened?"
- Clear Prompt: "What happened in the final scene of 'The Great Gatsby'?"

By mastering these basic concepts and techniques, you'll be able to craft effective prompts that yield high-quality responses from generative AI models. This foundational knowledge will set the stage for more advanced prompt engineering strategies.

Crafting Simple Prompts with Code

To effectively craft simple prompts and interact with generative AI models using code, you can leverage various AI APIs and libraries. Here's a step-by-step guide using Python, which includes setting up the environment, crafting prompts, and generating responses.

Setting Up the Environment

1. **Install Required Libraries:**

- Install the OpenAI library for accessing OpenAI's models.
- Install the **transformers** library for using Hugging Face models.

pip install openai transformers

1. **Set Up API Keys:**

- Obtain API keys from the respective platforms (e.g., OpenAI).
- Store them securely, possibly in environment variables or configuration files.

Example 1: Using OpenAI's GPT Models

1. **Import Libraries and Set Up API Key:**

```
import openai

import os

# Load your API key from an environment variable or a secure location

openai.api_key = os.getenv('OPENAI_API_KEY')
```

Crafting and Sending Simple Prompts:

```
def generate_response(prompt):

    response = openai.Completion.create(

        engine="text-davinci-003",

        prompt=prompt,

        max_tokens=100,
```

```
    temperature=0.7

)

    return response.choices[0].text.strip()


# Example prompts

simple_prompts = [

    "What is the capital of France?",

    "Explain the benefits of regular exercise.",

    "Write a short story about a heroic dog."

]

for prompt in simple_prompts:

    print(f"Prompt: {prompt}")

    print(f"Response: {generate_response(prompt)}\n")
```

Output: The AI will generate responses based on the prompts provided.

Prompt: What is the capital of France?

Response: The capital of France is Paris.

Prompt: Explain the benefits of regular exercise.

Response: Regular exercise improves cardiovascular health, boosts mental well-being, helps maintain a healthy weight, and strengthens muscles and bones.

Prompt: Write a short story about a heroic dog.

Response: Once upon a time, in a small village, there was a brave dog named Max. One day, a fire broke out in a house, and Max, sensing danger, rushed inside to save a child trapped in a room. His heroic actions earned him the admiration and gratitude of the entire village.

Example 2: Using Hugging Face Transformers

1. **Import Libraries and Load Model:**

```
from transformers import pipeline

# Load a pre-trained model for text generation

generator = pipeline('text-generation', model='gpt2')
```

Crafting and Sending Simple Prompts:

```
def generate_response(prompt):
    responses = generator(prompt, max_length=100, num_return_sequences=1)
    return responses[0]['generated_text']


# Example prompts

simple_prompts = [
    "What is the capital of France?",
    "Explain the benefits of regular exercise.",
```

"Write a short story about a heroic dog."

]

for prompt in simple_prompts:

   print(f"Prompt: {prompt}")

   print(f"Response: {generate_response(prompt)}\n")

Output: The AI will generate responses based on the prompts provided.

Prompt: What is the capital of France?

Response: The capital of France is Paris. It is known for its art, fashion, and culture.

Prompt: Explain the benefits of regular exercise.

Response: Regular exercise has numerous benefits including improving cardiovascular health, enhancing mental health, aiding weight loss, and building stronger muscles and bones. It can also help reduce the risk of chronic diseases such as diabetes and hypertension.

Prompt: Write a short story about a heroic dog.

Response: Once upon a time, there was a heroic dog named Rex. Rex was not just an ordinary dog; he had a keen sense of danger. One night, a fire broke out in his owner's house. Without hesitation, Rex ran through the smoke-filled rooms, barking loudly to wake everyone up. He led his family to safety, becoming the hero of the day.

Best Practices for Crafting Simple Prompts

- **Be Direct:** Use straightforward language to ensure the model understands your request.

- Example: Instead of "Can you maybe tell me what the capital of France is?" use "What is the capital of France?"

- **Specify the Task:** Clearly state what you want the AI to do.

- Example: Instead of "Write something about a dog," use "Write a short story about a heroic dog."

- **Test and Refine:** Experiment with different phrasings and refine the prompts based on the responses you receive.

- Example: Start with "Describe exercise benefits," then refine to "Explain the benefits of regular exercise."

By following these guidelines and using the provided code examples, you can effectively craft simple prompts and interact with generative AI models to generate high-quality responses.

Exploring AI Responses

Understanding and analyzing the responses generated by AI models is crucial for refining prompts and achieving desired outcomes. Here, we will explore how to interpret and improve AI-generated responses.

Analyzing AI Responses

1. **Relevance:** Determine if the response directly addresses the prompt.

- **Prompt:** "What are the benefits of regular exercise?"
- **Response:** "Regular exercise improves cardiovascular health, boosts mental well-being, and enhances physical fitness."
- **Analysis:** The response is relevant as it lists specific benefits of regular exercise.

2. **Coherence:** Check if the response is logical and well-organized.

- **Prompt:** "Write a short story about a heroic dog."
- **Response:** "Once upon a time, in a small village, there was a brave dog named Max. One day, a fire broke out in a house, and Max, sensing danger, rushed inside to save a child trapped in a room. His heroic actions earned him the admiration and gratitude of the entire village."
- **Analysis:** The response is coherent, with a clear beginning, middle, and end.

3. **Completeness:** Evaluate if the response fully answers the prompt.

- **Prompt:** "Explain the Pythagorean theorem."
- **Response:** "The Pythagorean theorem states that in a right-angled triangle, the square of the hypotenuse is equal to the sum of the squares of the other two sides."
- **Analysis:** The response is complete, providing the definition of the theorem.

4. **Accuracy:** Ensure the information provided is correct.

- **Prompt:** "Who was the first president of the United States?"
- **Response:** "The first president of the United States was George Washington."
- **Analysis:** The response is accurate.

Refining Prompts Based on Responses

1. **Identify Issues in the Response:**

- **Prompt:** "Tell me about Mars."
- **Response:** "Mars is the fourth planet from the Sun. It is known for its red color."
- **Issue:** The response is too brief and lacks depth.

2. **Refine the Prompt to Address Issues:**

- **Refined Prompt:** "Provide a detailed description of Mars, including its atmosphere, surface features, and potential for human exploration."
- **Expected Response:** "Mars, the fourth planet from the Sun, is known for its red color due to iron oxide on its surface. It has a thin atmosphere composed mostly of carbon dioxide, with traces of nitrogen and argon. Surface features include the largest volcano in the solar system, Olympus Mons, and the deep canyon Valles Marineris. Mars has been a focus of exploration due to its potential to support human life, with several missions investigating its surface and climate."

Using Code to Analyze and Refine AI Responses

1. **Initial Setup:**

```
import openai

import os

openai.api_key = os.getenv('OPENAI_API_KEY')

def generate_response(prompt):

    response = openai.Completion.create(

        engine="text-davinci-003",

        prompt=prompt,

        max_tokens=150,

        temperature=0.7

    )

    return response.choices[0].text.strip()
```

Generating and Analyzing Responses:

prompts = [

   "What are the benefits of regular exercise?",

   "Write a short story about a heroic dog.",

   "Explain the Pythagorean theorem.",

   "Tell me about Mars."

]

for prompt in prompts:

   response = generate_response(prompt)

   print(f"Prompt: {prompt}")

   print(f"Response: {response}\n")

Refining Prompts Based on Analysis:

refined_prompts = [

   "What are the physical, mental, and social benefits of regular exercise?",

   "Write a short story about a heroic dog who saves a child from a fire.",

   "Explain the Pythagorean theorem and provide an example calculation.",

   "Provide a detailed description of Mars, including its atmosphere, surface features, and potential for human exploration."

]

```
for prompt in refined_prompts:

    response = generate_response(prompt)

    print(f"Refined Prompt: {prompt}")

    print(f"Response: {response}\n")
```

Best Practices for Exploring AI Responses

1. **Iterative Refinement:** Continuously refine prompts based on the responses you receive to improve clarity and relevance.

2. **Contextual Prompts:** Provide sufficient context to guide the AI in generating more accurate and complete responses.

3. **Testing Variations:** Experiment with different phrasings and prompt structures to see which yields the best results.

4. **Feedback Loop:** Use the feedback from the responses to inform further prompt adjustments.

Example of an Iterative Refinement Process

1. **Initial Prompt and Response:**

- **Prompt:** "Tell me about the solar system."
- **Response:** "The solar system consists of the Sun and the objects that orbit it, including planets, moons, asteroids, and comets."

2. **Issue Identified:** The response is too general and lacks detail.

3. **Refined Prompt:**

- **Prompt:** "Describe the solar system in detail, including information about each planet and their characteristics."
- **Expected Response:** "The solar system consists of the Sun, eight planets, their moons, and other celestial objects like asteroids and comets. The planets are Mercury, Venus, Earth, Mars, Jupiter, Saturn, Uranus, and Neptune. Each planet has unique characteristics: Mercury is the smallest and closest to the Sun, Venus has a thick atmosphere and high surface temperatures, Earth supports life, Mars is known as the Red Planet, Jupiter is the largest, Saturn has prominent rings, Uranus has a tilted axis, and Neptune is known for its strong winds."

By systematically analyzing and refining AI responses, you can enhance the quality and relevance of the outputs, ensuring they meet your expectations and requirements.

Introduction to Parameters and Modifiers

Parameters and modifiers play a crucial role in shaping the responses generated by AI models. By adjusting these settings, you can fine-tune the output to meet specific requirements, control the creativity of responses, and ensure the results align more closely with your expectations.

Key Parameters

1. **Temperature:**

- **Definition:** Controls the randomness of the output. Lower values make the output more deterministic and focused, while higher values introduce more randomness and creativity.
- **Range:** Typically between 0.0 and 1.0.
- **Example Usage:**

    response = openai.Completion.create(engine="text-davinci-003", prompt="Write a creative story about a space adventure.", temperature=0.9)

2. **Max Tokens:**

- **Definition:** Limits the length of the generated response. One token generally corresponds to a word or part of a word.
- **Example Usage:**

  response = openai.Completion.create(engine="text-davinci-003", prompt="Summarize the plot of 'Pride and Prejudice'.", max_tokens=50)

3. **Top-p (Nucleus Sampling):**

- **Definition:** Controls the diversity of the output by considering only the top probability tokens whose cumulative probability is greater than or equal to the top-p value. Lower values keep the response more focused, while higher values allow more variability.
- **Range:** Between 0.0 and 1.0.
- **Example Usage:**

  response = openai.Completion.create(

  engine="text-davinci-003",

  prompt="Generate a list of creative business ideas.",

  top_p=0.8

Frequency Penalty:

- **Definition:** Discourages the model from repeating words or phrases by assigning a penalty to frequently used tokens.
- **Range:** Between 0.0 and 2.0.
- **Example Usage:**

  response = openai.Completion.create(

  engine="text-davinci-003",

  prompt="Describe the features of a smartphone.",

  frequency_penalty=0.5

)

Presence Penalty:

- **Definition:** Encourages the model to include new, non-repetitive information by assigning a penalty to already present tokens.
- **Range:** Between 0.0 and 2.0.
- **Example Usage:**

```
response = openai.Completion.create(

    engine="text-davinci-003",

    prompt="List some innovative uses for AI technology.",

    presence_penalty=0.6

)
```

Using Modifiers

Modifiers help tailor the tone, style, and context of the AI's response, making it more aligned with your specific needs.

1. **Tone and Style:**

- **Formal Tone:**

```
prompt = "Write a formal letter to a university requesting information about their computer science program."

response = openai.Completion.create(

    engine="text-davinci-003",

    prompt=prompt,
```

temperature=0.5

)

Casual Tone:

prompt = "Write a casual email to a friend about your vacation."

response = openai.Completion.create(

    engine="text-davinci-003",

    prompt=prompt,

    temperature=0.7

)

2. **Contextual Information:**

- **Adding Background Context:**

prompt = "As an AI language model developed by OpenAI, write a paragraph explaining the impact of AI on education."

response = openai.Completion.create(

    engine="text-davinci-003",

    prompt=prompt,

    temperature=0.5

)

3. **Role-Based Modifiers:**

- **Role-Playing Scenarios:**

prompt = "You are a fitness coach. Explain the importance of a balanced diet to your client."

response = openai.Completion.create(

   engine="text-davinci-003",

   prompt=prompt,

   temperature=0.6

)

   4. **Instructions for Specific Output:**

- **Structured Output:**

prompt = "Provide a step-by-step guide on how to bake a chocolate cake."

response = openai.Completion.create(

   engine="text-davinci-003",

   prompt=prompt,

   temperature=0.4

)

Example: Combining Parameters and Modifiers

Here's an example of combining different parameters and modifiers to tailor the response of the AI model:

import openai

import os

```python
openai.api_key = os.getenv('OPENAI_API_KEY')

def generate_response(prompt, temperature=0.7, max_tokens=150, top_p=0.9, frequency_penalty=0.5, presence_penalty=0.5):
    response = openai.Completion.create(
        engine="text-davinci-003",
        prompt=prompt,
        temperature=temperature,
        max_tokens=max_tokens,
        top_p=top_p,
        frequency_penalty=frequency_penalty,
        presence_penalty=presence_penalty
    )
    return response.choices[0].text.strip()


# Example prompt with modifiers
prompt = "You are a historian. Explain the significance of the Renaissance period in Europe."

response = generate_response(prompt, temperature=0.6, max_tokens=200, top_p=0.8, frequency_penalty=0.4, presence_penalty=0.4)

print(f"Response: {response}")
```

Output:

The AI will generate a detailed, historically accurate response about the Renaissance period.

By understanding and utilizing parameters and modifiers, you can effectively control and refine the outputs of generative AI models, ensuring they meet specific requirements and deliver high-quality results.

Techniques for Effective Prompt Design

Prompt Templates

Prompt templates provide a structured format for generating text using language models like GPT-3 or LLama. These templates guide the model by providing a specific context or outline, which helps generate more relevant and coherent responses. Here are some common types of prompt templates:

1. Question-Answer Templates:

These templates are used to generate answers to specific questions. The prompt typically includes the question followed by placeholders for the answer.

Example:
Question: What is the capital of France?
Answer: Paris

2. Dialogue Templates:

Dialogue templates simulate a conversation between two or more parties. They provide prompts for each participant's dialogue turn.

Example:
Speaker 1: Hi, how are you?
Speaker 2: I'm doing well, thank you for asking. How about you?

3. Story Starters:

Story starter templates provide the beginning of a narrative or story, prompting the model to continue the storyline.

Example:
Once upon a time, in a faraway kingdom,

4. Fill-in-the-Blank Templates:

These templates contain a sentence with one or more blanks to be filled in by the model.

Example:
The best part about summer is _____.

5. Command Templates:

Command templates instruct the model to perform a specific action or task.

Example:
Create a poem about love.

6. Comparison Templates:

These templates ask the model to compare two or more items, concepts, or ideas.

Example:
Compare and contrast cats and dogs.

7. Opinion Templates:

Opinion templates solicit the model's opinion on a given topic.

Example:
What do you think about artificial intelligence?

8. Instruction Templates:
Instruction templates provide step-by-step instructions for completing a task.

Example:

How to bake a chocolate cake:
1. Preheat the oven to 350°F.
2. ...

9. Problem-Solution Templates:

These templates outline a problem and ask the model to propose a solution.

Example:
Problem: Traffic congestion in urban areas.
Solution: Implementing public transportation and carpooling initiatives.

10. Reflection Templates:

Reflection templates prompt the model to reflect on a past experience or event.

Example:
Reflect on a memorable vacation you've had.

11. Argument Templates:

Argument templates present a topic and ask the model to provide arguments supporting or opposing it.

Example:
Topic: Should homework be abolished?
Arguments in favor: ...
Arguments against: ...

Note:
When using prompt templates, it's essential to provide clear and concise instructions to guide the model effectively. Experiment

with different templates and adjust them based on the desired output and the specific capabilities of the language model being used.

Few-Shot and Zero-Shot Learning

Few-shot learning and zero-shot learning are machine learning techniques that aim to train models to perform tasks with limited or no labeled data, respectively. Let's explore each concept:

Few-Shot Learning:

Few-shot learning refers to the process of training a model with only a small number of labeled examples per class. Traditional machine learning approaches require a large amount of labeled data to achieve good performance, but in real-world scenarios, collecting such data can be expensive or impractical. Few-shot learning addresses this limitation by enabling models to learn from a few examples.

Techniques in Few-Shot Learning:

1. **Transfer Learning**: Transfer knowledge from a pre-trained model on a large dataset to a new task with limited data.

2. **Meta-Learning**: Train a model to learn how to learn, where it becomes adept at adapting to new tasks with minimal data.

3. **Data Augmentation**: Generate additional training examples by applying transformations to existing data, effectively increasing the size of the training set.

4. **Fine-Tuning**: Fine-tune a pre-trained model on a small dataset to adapt it to a specific task or domain.

Zero-Shot Learning:

Zero-shot learning goes a step further than few-shot learning and aims to perform tasks without any labeled examples of the target classes during training. Instead, zero-shot learning models rely on auxiliary information, such as class descriptions or semantic embeddings, to generalize to unseen classes at inference time.

Techniques in Zero-Shot Learning:

1. **Semantic Embeddings**: Represent classes and features in a continuous semantic space, allowing the model to reason about unseen classes based on their semantic similarity to known classes.

2. **Attribute-Based Learning**: Describe classes using a set of attributes or semantic features, enabling the model to recognize new classes based on shared attributes.

3. **Transductive Learning**: Use both labeled and unlabeled data during training to improve the model's ability to generalize to unseen classes.

4. **Generative Models**: Train generative models to synthesize examples of unseen classes, bridging the gap between seen and unseen data distributions.

Comparison:

- **Data Requirement**: Few-shot learning requires a small amount of labeled data per class, while zero-shot learning operates with no labeled data for unseen classes.

- **Generalization**: Few-shot learning aims to generalize to new examples of known classes, whereas zero-shot learning focuses on generalizing to unseen classes.

- **Auxiliary Information**: Few-shot learning typically relies on labeled examples, while zero-shot learning leverages auxiliary information or attributes to reason about unseen classes.

- **Applications**: Few-shot learning is applicable in scenarios where limited labeled data is available, while zero-shot learning is useful for tasks involving novel or unseen classes.

Certainly! Let's delve into implementations of Few-Shot Learning and Zero-Shot Learning with code examples using Python and popular machine learning libraries like TensorFlow and PyTorch.

Few-Shot Learning with Prototypical Networks (PyTorch):

Prototypical Networks are a popular few-shot learning approach introduced by Snell et al. They learn a metric space where examples from the same class are closer to each other than to examples from different classes.

```python
import torch
import torch.nn as nn
import torch.optim as optim
from torchvision import datasets, transforms
from torch.utils.data import DataLoader
from torchvision.models import resnet18

# Define Prototypical Network
class PrototypicalNet(nn.Module):
    def __init__(self, num_input_channels, num_output_channels):
        super(PrototypicalNet, self).__init__()
        self.encoder = resnet18(pretrained=True)
        self.encoder.fc = nn.Identity()  # Remove the final fully connected layer
        self.prototypes = nn.Linear(num_input_channels, num_output_channels)

    def forward(self, x):
        x = self.encoder(x)
        x = x.view(x.size(0), -1)
        x = self.prototypes(x)
        return x

# Few-shot learning setup
num_classes = 5
num_support_examples_per_class = 5
num_query_examples_per_class = 5
num_input_channels = 512  # Depends on the output channels of the ResNet backbone
num_output_channels = num_classes
```

```
# Initialize Prototypical Network
prototypical_net = PrototypicalNet(num_input_channels, num_output_channels)

# Define loss function and optimizer
criterion = nn.CrossEntropyLoss()
optimizer = optim.SGD(prototypical_net.parameters(), lr=0.001, momentum=0.9)

# Load data (e.g., from Omniglot dataset)
transform = transforms.Compose([transforms.ToTensor()])
train_dataset = datasets.Omniglot(root='./data', download=True, transform=transform)
train_dataloader = DataLoader(train_dataset, batch_size=num_classes, shuffle=True)

# Training loop
num_epochs = 10
for epoch in range(num_epochs):
    for batch_idx, (data, targets) in enumerate(train_dataloader):
        optimizer.zero_grad()
        prototypes = prototypical_net(data)
        prototypes = prototypes.view(num_classes, num_support_examples_per_class, num_output_channels)
        prototypes = torch.mean(prototypes, dim=1)  # Compute prototypes as the mean of support examples
        prototypes = prototypes.unsqueeze(0).repeat(num_classes, 1, 1)  # Repeat prototypes for each query example
        outputs = prototypes.view(-1, num_output_channels)
        targets = targets.repeat(num_query_examples_per_class)
        loss = criterion(outputs, targets)
        loss.backward()
        optimizer.step()
        print(f'Epoch [{epoch+1}/{num_epochs}], Batch [{batch_idx+1}/{len(train_dataloader)}], Loss: {loss.item():.4f}')
```

Zero-Shot Learning with Semantic Embeddings (TensorFlow):

Zero-shot learning with semantic embeddings involves representing classes and features in a continuous semantic space. In this example, we'll use pre-trained word embeddings to perform zero-shot image classification.

```python
import numpy as np
import tensorflow as tf
from tensorflow.keras.applications import ResNet50
from tensorflow.keras.applications.resnet50 import preprocess_input, decode_predictions
from tensorflow.keras.layers import Input, Dense
from tensorflow.keras.models import Model
from gensim.models import KeyedVectors

# Load pre-trained word embeddings (e.g., Word2Vec)
word_embeddings = KeyedVectors.load_word2vec_format('path/to/word_embeddings.bin', binary=True)

# Define ResNet50 as the image feature extractor
image_input = Input(shape=(224, 224, 3))
resnet = ResNet50(include_top=False, weights='imagenet', input_tensor=image_input)

# Freeze ResNet50 layers
for layer in resnet.layers:
    layer.trainable = False

# Define zero-shot learning model
x = resnet.output
x = tf.keras.layers.GlobalAveragePooling2D()(x)
x = Dense(512, activation='relu')(x)
predictions = Dense(len(word_embeddings.vocab), activation='softmax')(x)

model = Model(inputs=resnet.input, outputs=predictions)
model.compile(optimizer='adam', loss='categorical_crossentropy', metrics=['accuracy'])

# Load and preprocess images
# (Code for loading and preprocessing images is omitted for brevity)

# Perform zero-shot classification
image_features = model.predict(preprocess_input(images))

# Compute cosine similarity between image features and word embeddings
similarity_scores = np.dot(image_features, word_embeddings.vectors.T)
```

```
predicted_classes = [word_embeddings.index2word[idx] for idx
in np.argmax(similarity_scores, axis=1)]
```

In both examples, we demonstrate how to implement Few-Shot Learning and Zero-Shot Learning using Prototypical Networks and Semantic Embeddings, respectively. Adjustments may be needed based on your specific dataset and task requirements.

Applications of Prompt Engineering

Chatbots and Virtual Assistants Using Prompt Engineering

Prompt engineering is a critical aspect of developing chatbots and virtual assistants, especially when using advanced language models like OpenAI's GPT-3, GPT-4, or Meta's LLaMA. This approach involves designing prompts that effectively guide the model to generate desired responses. Below, we'll explore the process and provide a code example using OpenAI's GPT-3.5 API.

Key Concepts in Prompt Engineering for Chatbots

1. **Prompt Design**: Crafting prompts that include context, instructions, and examples to steer the model towards producing relevant outputs.

2. **Context Management**: Maintaining the conversation context across multiple turns.

3. **Dynamic Prompting**: Adjusting prompts based on user inputs and conversation state.

4. **Error Handling**: Designing prompts to handle misunderstandings and incorrect responses gracefully

Example: Building a Simple Chatbot with GPT-3.5

Step 1: Setting Up

First, you need to install the OpenAI Python client and set up your environment:

pip install openai

Step 2: Writing the Code

Here's a Python example that demonstrates how to create a simple chatbot using GPT-3.5 and prompt engineering:

```python
import openai

# Initialize the OpenAI API key
openai.api_key = 'your-api-key'

def generate_prompt(user_input, chat_history):
    # Construct the prompt with chat history and the user's latest input
    prompt = "You are a helpful and friendly chatbot.\n"
    for interaction in chat_history:
        prompt += f"User: {interaction['user']}\nBot: {interaction['bot']}\n"
    prompt += f"User: {user_input}\nBot:"
    return prompt

def get_response(user_input, chat_history):
    # Generate a prompt with the current context
    prompt = generate_prompt(user_input, chat_history)

    # Call the OpenAI API to get a response
    response = openai.Completion.create(
        engine="text-davinci-003",
        prompt=prompt,
        max_tokens=150,
        n=1,
        stop=["\nUser:", "\nBot:"]
    )

    # Extract the response text
    bot_response = response.choices[0].text.strip()

    return bot_response
```

```
# Example chat history
chat_history = [
    {"user": "Hello!", "bot": "Hi there! How can I help you today?"},
    {"user": "Can you tell me a joke?", "bot": "Sure! Why don't scientists trust atoms? Because they make up everything!"}
]

# User input
user_input = "What's the weather like today?"

# Get bot response
bot_response = get_response(user_input, chat_history)
print(f"Bot: {bot_response}")

# Update chat history
chat_history.append({"user": user_input, "bot": bot_response})
```

Detailed Explanation

1. **Initialization**: We start by initializing the OpenAI API with your API key.

2. **Prompt Generation**:

- **generate_prompt**: This function constructs the prompt for the model. It includes a basic instruction ("You are a helpful and friendly chatbot") and appends the conversation history along with the latest user input.

3. **Getting a Response**:

- **get_response**: This function generates the complete prompt, calls the OpenAI API, and retrieves the response. The **stop** parameter is used to define when the model should stop generating text to avoid unwanted continuations.

4. **Chat History Management**:

- The chat history is maintained as a list of dictionaries, where each entry contains the user input and the corresponding bot response.

Advanced Prompt Engineering Techniques

1. **Dynamic Prompts**: Adjust the prompts based on user input patterns or specific keywords to make the chatbot more responsive and context-aware.

2. **Few-Shot Learning**: Include examples of good conversations in the prompt to guide the model towards producing similar responses.

    ```
    def generate_prompt(user_input, chat_history):
        examples = """
        User: Hi, what's your name?
        Bot: I'm your virtual assistant. How can I help you today?
        User: Can you recommend a book?
        Bot: Sure! I recommend 'To Kill a Mockingbird' by Harper Lee. It's a classic!
        """

        prompt = f"{examples}\n"
        for interaction in chat_history:
            prompt += f"User: {interaction['user']}\nBot: {interaction['bot']}\n"
        prompt += f"User: {user_input}\nBot:"
        return prompt
    ```

3. **Error Handling**: Design prompts to handle misunderstandings and prompt the user for more information if the model's response is unclear.

    ```
    def get_response(user_input, chat_history):
        prompt = generate_prompt(user_input, chat_history)

        response = openai.Completion.create(
            engine="text-davinci-003",
            prompt=prompt,
            max_tokens=150,
            n=1,
            stop=["\nUser:", "\nBot:"]
        )

        bot_response = response.choices[0].text.strip()

        if not bot_response:
    ```

        bot_response = "I'm sorry, I didn't quite catch that. Could you please rephrase?"

    return bot_response

Conclusion

Prompt engineering is a powerful technique in the development of chatbots and virtual assistants, leveraging the capabilities of advanced language models. By designing effective prompts, managing conversation context, and handling errors gracefully, you can create more interactive and user-friendly chatbots. This example provides a foundational approach, and you can expand upon it by integrating more complex NLP techniques and external data sources.

Content Creation Tools

Creating content using prompt engineering involves leveraging advanced language models like GPT-3.5 or GPT-4 to generate high-quality text for various purposes, such as blog posts, social media updates, marketing copy, and more. Below, I'll describe how to create content creation tools using prompt engineering, accompanied by code examples.

Key Concepts in Prompt Engineering for Content Creation

1. **Prompt Design**: Crafting prompts that include clear instructions, context, and examples to guide the model in generating the desired content.

2. **Template-based Prompts**: Using templates to standardize the structure of the generated content.

3. **Dynamic Content Generation**: Adjusting prompts based on specific requirements such as tone, style, and length.

4. **Iterative Refinement**: Generating multiple drafts and refining them for quality and accuracy.

Example: Creating a Blog Post Generator

Step 1: Setting Up
First, ensure you have the OpenAI Python client installed and set up your environment:

pip install openai

Step 2: Writing the Code
Here's a Python example that demonstrates how to create a content generation tool for blog posts using GPT-3.5:

```python
import openai

# Initialize the OpenAI API key
openai.api_key = 'your-api-key'

def generate_prompt(topic, keywords, tone, length):
    # Construct the prompt with detailed instructions and context
    prompt = (f"Write a blog post about '{topic}'. "
              f"Include the following keywords: {', '.join(keywords)}. "
              f"The tone of the article should be {tone}. "
              f"The length should be approximately {length} words.\n\n"
              "Start the article with an engaging introduction, then follow with detailed content, "
              "and end with a conclusion that wraps up the topic.\n\n"
              "Title: ")
    return prompt

def get_blog_post(topic, keywords, tone, length):
    # Generate the prompt
    prompt = generate_prompt(topic, keywords, tone, length)

    # Call the OpenAI API to generate the blog post
    response = openai.Completion.create(
        engine="text-davinci-003",
        prompt=prompt,
        max_tokens=length * 4,  # Adjust based on word-to-token ratio
        n=1,
        stop=None,
        temperature=0.7  # Adjust temperature for creativity
    )
```

```
# Extract the response text
blog_post = response.choices[0].text.strip()

return blog_post

# Example usage
topic = "The Benefits of a Healthy Lifestyle"
keywords = ["nutrition", "exercise", "mental health"]
tone = "informative"
length = 500  # Length in words

blog_post = get_blog_post(topic, keywords, tone, length)
print(blog_post)
```

Detailed Explanation

1. **Initialization**: Set up the OpenAI API with your API key.

2. **Prompt Generation**:

- **generate_prompt**: This function constructs a detailed prompt, specifying the topic, keywords, tone, and length. Clear instructions guide the model to generate a well-structured blog post.

3. **Content Generation**:

- **get_blog_post**: This function calls the OpenAI API with the generated prompt. The **max_tokens** parameter is adjusted based on the desired length of the blog post, considering that one word is roughly 4 tokens on average.

4. **Example Usage**: The example demonstrates how to generate a blog post about "The Benefits of a Healthy Lifestyle" with specific keywords, tone, and length.

Advanced Content Creation Techniques

1. **Template-based Prompts**: Define different templates for various types of content, such as product descriptions, social media posts, or email newsletters.

```python
def generate_social_media_prompt(product_name, key_features, call_to_action):
    prompt = (f"Create a social media post for a product called '{product_name}'. "
              f"Highlight the following features: {', '.join(key_features)}. "
              f"End the post with a call to action: '{call_to_action}'.\n\n"
              "Post: ")
    return prompt
```

2. **Dynamic Content Generation**: Adjust prompts dynamically based on user input to generate content in different styles or formats.

```python
def generate_dynamic_prompt(content_type, topic, audience, tone):
    prompt = (f"Create a {content_type} about '{topic}' for a {audience} audience. "
              f"The tone should be {tone}. Provide engaging and informative content.\n\n"
              "Content: ")
    return prompt

content_type = "newsletter"
topic = "New Features in Our Product"
audience = "existing customers"
tone = "excited"

dynamic_prompt = generate_dynamic_prompt(content_type, topic, audience, tone)
```

3. **Iterative Refinement**: Generate multiple drafts and refine them to improve quality.

```python
def refine_content(draft, feedback):
    prompt = (f"Here is a draft of the content:\n{draft}\n\n"
              f"Based on the following feedback, improve the content:\n{feedback}\n\n"
              "Revised content: ")
    response = openai.Completion.create(
        engine="text-davinci-003",
        prompt=prompt,
        max_tokens=500,
```

```
    n=1,
    stop=None,
    temperature=0.7
)
refined_content = response.choices[0].text.strip()
return refined_content
```

draft = "Our product now includes several new features."
feedback = "Make the content more engaging and detailed."
refined_content = refine_content(draft, feedback)
print(refined_content)

Conclusion

Prompt engineering is a powerful technique for creating content generation tools. By designing effective prompts, utilizing templates, dynamically generating content, and iteratively refining drafts, you can create versatile tools that produce high-quality content for various applications. The provided examples offer a foundation, and you can expand upon them to suit specific needs and contexts.

Interactive AI Systems

Interactive AI systems are designed to engage users in meaningful, dynamic interactions. These systems leverage advanced natural language processing (NLP) models, like OpenAI's GPT-3.5 or GPT-4, to understand and respond to user inputs effectively. Prompt engineering plays a crucial role in shaping these interactions by creating prompts that guide the AI to generate relevant and coherent responses.

Here's a detailed description and example code for building an interactive AI system using prompt engineering.

Key Concepts in Interactive AI Systems

1. **Prompt Engineering**: Crafting prompts that effectively guide the model to generate appropriate and contextually relevant responses.
2. **Context Management**: Maintaining the context of the conversation to ensure coherent interactions over multiple turns.
3. **Dynamic Response Generation**: Creating dynamic prompts that adapt based on user inputs and conversation flow.
4. **User Personalization**: Tailoring responses to individual users based on their preferences and previous interactions.
5. **Error Handling**: Designing prompts to handle misunderstandings and incorrect responses gracefully.

Example: Building an Interactive AI System

Step 1: Setting Up
First, ensure you have the OpenAI Python client installed and set up your environment:

pip install openai

Step 2: Writing the Code
Here's a Python example demonstrating how to create an interactive AI system using GPT-3.5:

import openai

# Initialize the OpenAI API key
openai.api_key = 'your-api-key'

def generate_prompt(user_input, chat_history):
    # Construct the prompt with chat history and the user's latest input
    prompt = "You are a helpful and friendly AI assistant.\n"
    for interaction in chat_history:
        prompt += f"User: {interaction['user']}\nAI: {interaction['ai']}\n"
    prompt += f"User: {user_input}\nAI:"
    return prompt

def get_response(user_input, chat_history):
    # Generate a prompt with the current context

```
prompt = generate_prompt(user_input, chat_history)

# Call the OpenAI API to get a response
response = openai.Completion.create(
   engine="text-davinci-003",
   prompt=prompt,
   max_tokens=150,
   n=1,
   stop=["\nUser:", "\nAI:"]
)

# Extract the response text
ai_response = response.choices[0].text.strip()

return ai_response

# Example chat history
chat_history = [
   {"user": "Hello!", "ai": "Hi there! How can I assist you today?"},
   {"user": "Can you help me with my homework?", "ai": "Of course! What subject are you working on?"}
]

# User input
user_input = "I need help with math."

# Get AI response
ai_response = get_response(user_input, chat_history)
print(f"AI: {ai_response}")

# Update chat history
chat_history.append({"user": user_input, "ai": ai_response})
```

Detailed Explanation

1. **Initialization**: Set up the OpenAI API with your API key.

2. **Prompt Generation**:

- **generate_prompt**: This function constructs a detailed prompt, incorporating the conversation history and the user's latest input. The initial instruction ("You are a helpful and friendly AI assistant") guides the model to maintain a consistent and friendly tone.

3. **Context Management**:

- The prompt includes the entire conversation history to provide context, ensuring the AI's responses are relevant and coherent.

4. **Response Generation**:

- **get_response**: This function calls the OpenAI API with the generated prompt and retrieves the AI's response. The **max_tokens** parameter limits the length of the response, and the **stop** parameter ensures the response ends at a logical point.

5. **Chat History Management**:

- The chat history is maintained as a list of dictionaries, where each entry contains the user's input and the corresponding AI response.

Advanced Interactive AI Techniques

1. **Dynamic Response Generation**: Adjust prompts based on user input patterns or specific keywords to make the AI more responsive and context-aware.

    ```python
    def generate_dynamic_prompt(user_input, chat_history):
        prompt = "You are an AI assistant specializing in providing detailed and helpful responses.\n"
        for interaction in chat_history:
            prompt += f"User: {interaction['user']}\nAI: {interaction['ai']}\n"
        prompt += f"User: {user_input}\nAI:"
        return prompt
    ```

2. **User Personalization**: Tailor responses based on individual user preferences and previous interactions.

    ```
    user_profiles = {
        "user123": {"name": "Alice", "preferences": ["short responses", "tech news"]}
    }
    ```

```
def generate_personalized_prompt(user_id, user_input, chat_history):
    user_profile = user_profiles.get(user_id, {"name": "User", "preferences": []})
    prompt = f"You are an AI assistant. Address the user by their name, {user_profile['name']}.\n"
    for interaction in chat_history:
        prompt += f"{user_profile['name']}: {interaction['user']}\nAI: {interaction['ai']}\n"
    prompt += f"{user_profile['name']}: {user_input}\nAI:"
    return prompt
```

3. **Error Handling**: Design prompts to handle misunderstandings and guide the conversation back on track.

```
def get_response(user_input, chat_history):
    prompt = generate_prompt(user_input, chat_history)

    response = openai.Completion.create(
        engine="text-davinci-003",
        prompt=prompt,
        max_tokens=150,
        n=1,
        stop=["\nUser:", "\nAI:"]
    )

    ai_response = response.choices[0].text.strip()

    if not ai_response:
        ai_response = "I'm sorry, I didn't understand that. Could you please rephrase?"

    return ai_response
```

Conclusion

Interactive AI systems leverage prompt engineering to create dynamic and engaging user interactions. By designing effective prompts, managing conversation context, personalizing responses, and handling errors gracefully, you can build sophisticated AI assistants that provide meaningful interactions. The provided examples offer a foundational approach, and you can expand upon them to suit specific needs and applications.

Chapter 12 Retrieval-Augmented Generation (RAG) Framework

Retrieval-Augmented Generation (RAG) Framework

Retrieval-Augmented Generation (RAG) is an advanced framework that combines the strengths of retrieval-based and generation-based models to enhance the performance and accuracy of natural language processing (NLP) tasks. Developed by Facebook AI, RAG leverages both pre-trained generative models and external knowledge sources to produce more informative and contextually relevant responses.
Key Concepts

Retrieval-Based Models: These models fetch relevant information from a large corpus or database in response to a query. They excel at providing factual, specific, and contextually relevant data.

1. **Generative Models**: These models generate responses based on learned patterns from a training dataset. They are capable of producing coherent and contextually appropriate language, but might sometimes produce plausible-sounding but incorrect information.

2. **Combining Strengths**: RAG integrates these two approaches to utilize the vast knowledge base of retrieval models and the contextual language generation capabilities of generative models.

How RAG Works

1. **Query Retrieval:**

   - When a query is received, the system first uses a retriever model to search a large database or corpus for relevant documents or passages.
   - This step ensures that the system has access to pertinent information that might not be directly encoded within the generative model.

2. **Document Encoding:**

   - The retrieved documents are then encoded into a format that the generative model can understand. This often involves embedding the documents into a vector space using techniques like BERT or other transformer-based models.

3. **Response Generation:**

   - The generative model, typically a variant of the GPT or BART architecture, takes the encoded documents as context and generates a response.
   - This response is informed by both the retrieved documents and the generative model's inherent language capabilities, leading to more accurate and contextually relevant outputs.

4. **Output:**

   - The final output is a synthesized response that combines the precision of the retrieved information with the fluency and contextuality of the generative model.

Advantages of RAG

1. **Improved Accuracy**: By incorporating real-time retrieval of relevant information, RAG can provide more accurate and up-to-date responses.

2. **Contextual Relevance**: The combination of retrieval and generation ensures that responses are not only accurate but also contextually appropriate and coherent.

3. **Flexibility**: RAG can handle a wide range of tasks, from answering factual questions to engaging in more open-ended conversations.

4. **Scalability**: The framework can be scaled to include larger and more diverse datasets for retrieval, improving the breadth and depth of available knowledge.

Applications of RAG

1. **Question Answering Systems**: Enhancing QA systems by providing precise and contextually relevant answers.

2. **Customer Support**: Offering more accurate and helpful responses in customer service applications.

3. **Content Generation**: Assisting in generating content that requires up-to-date and factual information.

4. **Research Assistance**: Providing researchers with relevant information and summaries from large databases.

Example: Implementing a Simple RAG System

Here's a basic implementation of a RAG system using Python and Hugging Face's Transformers library. Note that this example is simplified and would need a more sophisticated setup for production use.

Step 1: Install Required Libraries

pip install transformers faiss-cpu

Step 2: Import Necessary Modules

```
from transformers import DPRQuestionEncoder, DPRContextEncoder, DPRReader, pipeline
import torch
import faiss
```

```python
# Initialize models
question_encoder = DPRQuestionEncoder.from_pretrained("facebook/dpr-question_encoder-single-nq-base")
context_encoder = DPRContextEncoder.from_pretrained("facebook/dpr-ctx_encoder-single-nq-base")
reader = DPRReader.from_pretrained("facebook/dpr-reader-single-nq-base")

# Initialize pipelines
retriever = pipeline("retrieval-based-query-answering", model="facebook/dpr-ctx_encoder-single-nq-base")
```

Step 3: Create a Sample Knowledge Base

```python
documents = [
    {"title": "Document 1", "text": "This is the text of the first document."},
    {"title": "Document 2", "text": "This is the text of the second document."},
    {"title": "Document 3", "text": "This is the text of the third document."}
]

# Encode documents
context_embeddings = context_encoder(
    **context_encoder.tokenizer([doc["text"] for doc in documents], return_tensors="pt", padding=True, truncation=True)
).pooler_output
```

Step 4: Create a FAISS Index for Efficient Retrieval

```python
index = faiss.IndexFlatL2(context_embeddings.shape[1])
index.add(context_embeddings.detach().numpy())
```
Step 5: Implement the Query Function

```python
def query_rag(question, top_k=1):
    # Encode the question
    question_embedding = question_encoder(**question_encoder.tokenizer(question, return_tensors="pt")).pooler_output

    # Retrieve relevant documents
```

```
    distances,                indices               =
index.search(question_embedding.detach().numpy(), top_k)
    retrieved_docs = [documents[i] for i in indices[0]]

    # Generate a response
    inputs = reader.tokenizer(
        questions=[question] * top_k,
        titles=[doc["title"] for doc in retrieved_docs],
        texts=[doc["text"] for doc in retrieved_docs],
        return_tensors="pt",
        padding=True,
        truncation=True
    )
    outputs = reader(**inputs)

    # Extract the best answer
    answer                                           =
reader.tokenizer.decode(outputs.start_logits.argmax(),
skip_special_tokens=True)
    return answer

# Example usage
question = "What is the text of the first document?"
answer = query_rag(question)
print(f"Answer: {answer}")
```

Conclusion

The Retrieval-Augmented Generation (RAG) framework represents a significant advancement in natural language processing by effectively combining retrieval-based and generation-based approaches. This hybrid method leverages the extensive knowledge base accessible through retrieval models and the sophisticated language capabilities of generative models, resulting in more accurate, relevant, and coherent responses. The example provided demonstrates a simplified implementation, showcasing the core concepts and benefits of the RAG framework.

Components of the Retrieval-Augmented Generation (RAG) Framework

The RAG framework integrates multiple components to combine the strengths of retrieval-based and generation-based models. Here, we will describe the key components involved in this framework:

1. **Retriever Model**
2. **Document Encoder**
3. **Generative Model**
4. **Retrieval Index**
5. **Context Management**

1. Retriever Model

The retriever model is responsible for fetching relevant information from a large corpus or database based on the input query. It typically employs transformer-based architectures such as Dense Passage Retrieval (DPR), which uses a dual encoder approach:

- **Question Encoder**: Encodes the input query into a dense vector representation.

- **Context Encoder**: Encodes documents from the corpus into dense vector representations.
  These embeddings are then used to retrieve the most relevant documents through similarity search.

2. Document Encoder

The document encoder transforms the retrieved documents into a format that can be utilized by the generative model. This usually involves converting the documents into dense vector representations or token embeddings that the generative model can process. Pre-trained models like BERT or RoBERTa are commonly used for this purpose.

3. Generative Model

The generative model is typically a transformer-based model like GPT-3, BART, or T5. It generates responses based on the context provided by the document encoder and the initial query. The generative model integrates the information retrieved from the corpus with its own language understanding capabilities to produce coherent and contextually relevant responses.

4. Retrieval Index

The retrieval index is a data structure used to store and efficiently search the dense vector representations of documents. FAISS (Facebook AI Similarity Search) is a popular library used for this purpose. It supports fast similarity search and clustering of dense vectors, enabling quick retrieval of relevant documents in response to a query.

5. Context Management

Context management involves maintaining the state of the conversation or task over multiple interactions. This ensures that the generated responses are coherent and relevant to the ongoing context. Techniques include:

- **Maintaining Conversation History**: Storing previous interactions and using them as part of the input to the generative model.

- **Dynamic Prompt Construction**: Creating prompts that incorporate past context and new queries dynamically.

Example: Implementing a Simple RAG System with Components

Here's an example demonstrating how to implement a basic RAG system, highlighting each component:

Step 1: Install Required Libraries

pip install transformers faiss-cpu

Step 2: Import Necessary Modules

from transformers import DPRQuestionEncoder, DPRContextEncoder, DPRReader, pipeline

```python
import torch
import faiss

# Initialize models
question_encoder = DPRQuestionEncoder.from_pretrained("facebook/dpr-question_encoder-single-nq-base")
context_encoder = DPRContextEncoder.from_pretrained("facebook/dpr-ctx_encoder-single-nq-base")
reader = DPRReader.from_pretrained("facebook/dpr-reader-single-nq-base")
```

Step 3: Create a Sample Knowledge Base and Encode Documents

```python
documents = [
    {"title": "Document 1", "text": "This is the text of the first document."},
    {"title": "Document 2", "text": "This is the text of the second document."},
    {"title": "Document 3", "text": "This is the text of the third document."}
]

# Encode documents
context_embeddings = context_encoder(
    **context_encoder_tokenizer([doc["text"] for doc in documents], return_tensors="pt", padding=True, truncation=True)
).pooler_output
```

Step 4: Create a FAISS Index for Efficient Retrieval

```python
index = faiss.IndexFlatL2(context_embeddings.shape[1])
index.add(context_embeddings.detach().numpy())
```

Step 5: Implement the Query Function with Context Management

```python
def generate_prompt(question, chat_history):
    prompt = "You are an AI assistant. Answer the following question based on the provided context.\n"
    for interaction in chat_history:
```

```python
    prompt += f"User: {interaction['user']}\nAI: {interaction['ai']}\n"
    prompt += f"User: {question}\nAI:"
    return prompt

def query_rag(question, chat_history, top_k=1):
    # Encode the question
    question_embedding = question_encoder(**question_encoder.tokenizer(question, return_tensors="pt")).pooler_output

    # Retrieve relevant documents
    distances, indices = index.search(question_embedding.detach().numpy(), top_k)
    retrieved_docs = [documents[i] for i in indices[0]]

    # Generate a response
    inputs = reader.tokenizer(
        questions=[question] * top_k,
        titles=[doc["title"] for doc in retrieved_docs],
        texts=[doc["text"] for doc in retrieved_docs],
        return_tensors="pt",
        padding=True,
        truncation=True
    )
    outputs = reader(**inputs)

    # Extract the best answer
    answer = reader.tokenizer.decode(outputs.start_logits.argmax(), skip_special_tokens=True)
    return answer

# Example usage
chat_history = []
question = "What is the text of the first document?"
answer = query_rag(question, chat_history)
print(f"AI: {answer}")

# Update chat history
chat_history.append({"user": question, "ai": answer})
```

Conclusion

The RAG framework is a powerful approach that leverages the strengths of both retrieval-based and generation-based models to enhance the performance and accuracy of NLP tasks. By understanding and implementing each component—retriever model, document encoder, generative model, retrieval index, and context management—you can create sophisticated systems capable of providing highly relevant and contextually appropriate responses. This example provides a foundation for building more advanced and scalable RAG-based applications.

Working Mechanism of Retrieval-Augmented Generation (RAG)

Retrieval-Augmented Generation (RAG) is a hybrid framework that combines retrieval-based models and generative models to create a system that can generate accurate and contextually relevant responses by leveraging a large corpus of external documents. Below, we'll describe the working mechanism of RAG and provide a code example to illustrate how it can be implemented.
Working Mechanism

1. **Query Encoding**: The user query is encoded into a dense vector representation using a question encoder.

2. **Document Retrieval**: The encoded query is used to retrieve the most relevant documents from a large corpus. This involves encoding the documents into dense vectors and using similarity search to find the closest matches to the query.

3. **Document Encoding**: The retrieved documents are encoded into a format that can be used by the generative model.

4. **Response Generation**: The generative model uses the encoded documents and the original query to generate a response. This response is informed by both the retrieved documents and the model's inherent language understanding capabilities.

5. **Context Management**: The conversation context is managed to ensure coherence in multi-turn interactions.

Step-by-Step Code Example

Step 1: Install Required Libraries

First, ensure you have the necessary libraries installed. You'll need the **transformers** library for the models and **faiss-cpu** for efficient similarity search.

```
pip install transformers faiss-cpu
```

Step 2: Import Necessary Modules

Import the relevant classes and functions from the **transformers** library and other necessary modules.

```
from transformers import DPRQuestionEncoder, DPRContextEncoder, DPRReader, AutoTokenizer, pipeline
import torch
import faiss

# Initialize models
question_encoder = DPRQuestionEncoder.from_pretrained("facebook/dpr-question_encoder-single-nq-base")
context_encoder = DPRContextEncoder.from_pretrained("facebook/dpr-ctx_encoder-single-nq-base")
reader = DPRReader.from_pretrained("facebook/dpr-reader-single-nq-base")
```

Step 3: Create a Sample Knowledge Base and Encode Documents

Define a small corpus of documents and encode them using the context encoder.

```
documents = [
    {"title": "Document 1", "text": "This is the text of the first document."},
```

{"title": "Document 2", "text": "This is the text of the second document."},
{"title": "Document 3", "text": "This is the text of the third document."}
]

# Encode documents
context_embeddings = context_encoder(
    **context_encoder.tokenizer([doc["text"] for doc in documents], return_tensors="pt", padding=True, truncation=True)
).pooler_output

# Create FAISS index for efficient retrieval
index = faiss.IndexFlatL2(context_embeddings.shape[1])
index.add(context_embeddings.detach().numpy())

Step 4: Implement the Query Function with Context Management

Define functions to generate prompts, encode queries, retrieve relevant documents, and generate responses.

```
def generate_prompt(question, chat_history):
    prompt = "You are an AI assistant. Answer the following question based on the provided context.\n"
    for interaction in chat_history:
        prompt += f"User: {interaction['user']}\nAI: {interaction['ai']}\n"
    prompt += f"User: {question}\nAI:"
    return prompt

def query_rag(question, chat_history, top_k=1):
    # Encode the question
    question_embedding = question_encoder(**question_encoder.tokenizer(question, return_tensors="pt")).pooler_output

    # Retrieve relevant documents
    distances, indices = index.search(question_embedding.detach().numpy(), top_k)
    retrieved_docs = [documents[i] for i in indices[0]]

    # Generate a response
    inputs = reader.tokenizer(
```

```
        questions=[question] * top_k,
        titles=[doc["title"] for doc in retrieved_docs],
        texts=[doc["text"] for doc in retrieved_docs],
        return_tensors="pt",
        padding=True,
        truncation=True
    )
    outputs = reader(**inputs)

    # Extract the best answer
    answer                                                    =
reader.tokenizer.decode(outputs.start_logits.argmax(),
skip_special_tokens=True)
    return answer

# Example usage
chat_history = []
question = "What is the text of the first document?"
answer = query_rag(question, chat_history)
print(f"AI: {answer}")

# Update chat history
chat_history.append({"user": question, "ai": answer})
```

Detailed Explanation

1. **Query Encoding**:

- The **question_encoder** encodes the user query into a dense vector representation. This step translates the natural language query into a numerical format that can be processed for similarity search.

    ```
    question_embedding                                       =
    question_encoder(**question_encoder.tokenizer(question,
    return_tensors="pt")).pooler_output
    ```

    Document Retrieval:

- The encoded query is compared against the pre-encoded document vectors using FAISS, which performs efficient similarity search to find the top relevant documents.

```
distances, indices = index.search(question_embedding.detach().numpy(), top_k)
retrieved_docs = [documents[i] for i in indices[0]]
```

Document Encoding:

- The **context_encoder** encodes the retrieved documents into dense vectors that will be fed into the generative model.

```
context_embeddings = context_encoder(
    **context_encoder.tokenizer([doc["text"] for doc in documents], return_tensors="pt", padding=True, truncation=True)
).pooler_output
```

Response Generation:

- The **DPRReader** (generative model) takes the encoded documents and the query to generate a contextually informed response.

```
inputs = reader.tokenizer(
    questions=[question] * top_k,
    tItles=[doc["title"] for doc in retrieved_docs],
    texts=[doc["text"] for doc in retrieved_docs],
    return_tensors="pt",
    padding=True,
    truncation=True
)
outputs = reader(**inputs)
answer = reader.tokenizer.decode(outputs.start_logits.argmax(), skip_special_tokens=True)
```

Context Management:

- The conversation history is maintained and incorporated into the prompt to ensure coherent multi-turn interactions.

```
chat_history.append({"user": question, "ai": answer})
```

Conclusion

The RAG framework effectively combines retrieval-based and generation-based models to provide more accurate and contextually relevant responses. By understanding and implementing each component—query encoding, document retrieval, document encoding, response generation, and context management—you can create a sophisticated system capable of handling complex NLP tasks. This code example provides a foundational approach that can be expanded and adapted for more advanced applications.

Implementing RAG in AI Systems

Implementing Retrieval-Augmented Generation (RAG) in AI systems involves creating a hybrid model that leverages both retrieval-based and generation-based approaches to produce accurate and contextually relevant responses. Below, we will go through the detailed steps to implement a RAG-based system, complete with code examples using Python and the Hugging Face Transformers library.

Steps to Implement RAG in AI Systems

1. **Setup and Installation**
2. **Document Preparation and Encoding**
3. **Building the Retrieval Index**
4. **Query Encoding and Document Retrieval**
5. **Response Generation**

Step 1: Setup and Installation

First, install the required libraries. You'll need the **transformers** library for the models and **faiss-cpu** for efficient similarity search.
 pip install transformers faiss-cpu

Step 2: Document Preparation and Encoding

Define a small corpus of documents and encode them using the context encoder.

```
from transformers import DPRContextEncoder, DPRQuestionEncoder, DPRReader, AutoTokenizer
import torch

# Define documents
documents = [
    {"title": "Document 1", "text": "This is the text of the first document."},
    {"title": "Document 2", "text": "This is the text of the second document."},
    {"title": "Document 3", "text": "This is the text of the third document."}
]

# Initialize context encoder and tokenizer
context_encoder = DPRContextEncoder.from_pretrained("facebook/dpr-ctx_encoder-single-nq-base")
context_tokenizer = AutoTokenizer.from_pretrained("facebook/dpr-ctx_encoder-single-nq-base")

# Encode documents
context_embeddings = []
for doc in documents:
    inputs = context_tokenizer(doc["text"], return_tensors="pt", padding=True, truncation=True)
    embedding = context_encoder(**inputs).pooler_output
    context_embeddings.append(embedding.detach().numpy())

context_embeddings = torch.tensor(context_embeddings).squeeze(1)
```

Step 3: Building the Retrieval Index

Create a FAISS index for efficient retrieval of documents based on the query embeddings.

```
import faiss

# Initialize FAISS index
```

```
dimension = context_embeddings.shape[1]
index = faiss.IndexFlatL2(dimension)
index.add(context_embeddings.numpy())
```

Step 4: Query Encoding and Document Retrieval

Encode the user query and retrieve the most relevant documents from the FAISS index.

```
# Initialize question encoder and tokenizer
question_encoder = DPRQuestionEncoder.from_pretrained("facebook/dpr-question_encoder-single-nq-base")
question_tokenizer = AutoTokenizer.from_pretrained("facebook/dpr-question_encoder-single-nq-base")

# Function to encode the query and retrieve documents
def retrieve_documents(query, top_k=1):
    inputs = question_tokenizer(query, return_tensors="pt")
    question_embedding = question_encoder(**inputs).pooler_output.detach().numpy()

    # Retrieve documents
    distances, indices = index.search(question_embedding, top_k)
    retrieved_docs = [documents[i] for i in indices[0]]

    return retrieved_docs

# Example query
query = "What is the text of the first document?"
retrieved_docs = retrieve_documents(query, top_k=2)
print(retrieved_docs)
```

Step 5: Response Generation

Use the DPR Reader model to generate a response based on the retrieved documents and the query.

```
# Initialize reader model and tokenizer
reader = DPRReader.from_pretrained("facebook/dpr-reader-single-nq-base")
```

```python
reader_tokenizer = AutoTokenizer.from_pretrained("facebook/dpr-reader-single-nq-base")

# Function to generate a response
def generate_response(query, retrieved_docs):
    questions = [query] * len(retrieved_docs)
    titles = [doc["title"] for doc in retrieved_docs]
    texts = [doc["text"] for doc in retrieved_docs]

    inputs = reader_tokenizer(
        questions=questions,
        titles=titles,
        texts=texts,
        return_tensors="pt",
        padding=True,
        truncation=True
    )

    outputs = reader(**inputs)
    start_logits = outputs.start_logits
    end_logits = outputs.end_logits
    answers = []

    for i in range(len(retrieved_docs)):
        answer_start = torch.argmax(start_logits[i])
        answer_end = torch.argmax(end_logits[i]) + 1
        answer = reader_tokenizer.decode(inputs.input_ids[i][answer_start:answer_end], skip_special_tokens=True)
        answers.append(answer)

    return answers

# Generate a response for the query
response = generate_response(query, retrieved_docs)
print(response)
```

Detailed Explanation

1. **Document Preparation and Encoding**:

- We define a list of documents and use the **DPRContextEncoder** to encode the text of each document into dense vector representations.

```
documents = [
    {"title": "Document 1", "text": "This is the text of the first document."},
    {"title": "Document 2", "text": "This is the text of the second document."},
    {"title": "Document 3", "text": "This is the text of the third document."}
]
context_embeddings = []
for doc in documents:
    inputs = context_tokenizer(doc["text"], return_tensors="pt", padding=True, truncation=True)
    embedding = context_encoder(**inputs).pooler_output
    context_embeddings.append(embedding.detach().numpy())
```

Building the Retrieval Index:

- The encoded document vectors are added to a FAISS index to enable efficient similarity search.

```
dimension = context_embeddings.shape[1]
index = faiss.IndexFlatL2(dimension)
index.add(context_embeddings.numpy())
```

Query Encoding and Document Retrieval:

- The user query is encoded using the **DPRQuestionEncoder**, and the FAISS index is used to retrieve the most relevant documents based on the encoded query.

```
def retrieve_documents(query, top_k=1):
    inputs = question_tokenizer(query, return_tensors="pt")
    question_embedding = question_encoder(**inputs).pooler_output.detach().numpy()
    
    distances, indices = index.search(question_embedding, top_k)
    retrieved_docs = [documents[i] for i in indices[0]]
```

return retrieved_docs

Response Generation:

- The **DPRReader** model is used to generate a response. It takes the query and the retrieved documents as input and produces an answer based on the context provided by the documents.

```
def generate_response(query, retrieved_docs):
   questions = [query] * len(retrieved_docs)
   titles = [doc["title"] for doc in retrieved_docs]
   texts = [doc["text"] for doc in retrieved_docs]

   inputs = reader_tokenizer(
      questions=questions,
      titles=titles,
      texts=texts,
      return_tensors="pt",
      padding=True,
      truncation=True
   )

   outputs = reader(**inputs)
   start_logits = outputs.start_logits
   end_logits = outputs.end_logits
   answers = []

   for i in range(len(retrieved_docs)):
      answer_start = torch.argmax(start_logits[i])
      answer_end = torch.argmax(end_logits[i]) + 1
      answer = reader_tokenizer.decode(inputs.input_ids[i][answer_start:answer_end], skip_special_tokens=True)
      answers.append(answer)

   return answers
```

Conclusion

By following these steps, you can implement a Retrieval-Augmented Generation (RAG) system that combines retrieval-based and generation-based approaches to generate accurate and contextually relevant responses. This example provides a foundational understanding of how to build and integrate the components of the RAG framework using Python and Hugging Face's Transformers library.

Chapter 13 Future Directions and Emerging Trends

Future directions and emerging trends in generative AI encompass the evolving landscape of research, development, and application of AI technologies aimed at generating content, simulating human-like behaviours, and enhancing creativity. Here are some potential future directions and emerging trends in this field:

1. **Advancements in Model Architectures**:
   - Continued development of more sophisticated and efficient generative models, including novel architectures such as Transformers, BigGAN, and VQ-VAE-2, capable of generating high-quality and diverse content across different modalities (e.g., images, text, audio).

2. **Multimodal Generative Models**:
   - Integration of multiple modalities (e.g., text, images, audio) within generative models to enable the creation of multimodal content and facilitate more immersive and interactive user experiences.

3. **Ethical AI and Responsible Innovation**:
   - Greater emphasis on ethical considerations, fairness, transparency, and accountability in the development and deployment of generative AI technologies, along with the adoption of responsible innovation practices to mitigate potential risks and biases.

4. **Interpretability and Explainability**:
   - Research into methods for enhancing the interpretability and explainability of generative models,

enabling users to understand and interpret the underlying processes and decisions made by AI systems.

5. **Controlled Generation and Fine-Grained Manipulation:**
   - Advancements in techniques for controlling and manipulating the outputs of generative models, allowing users to specify desired attributes, styles, or characteristics of the generated content with greater precision and control.

6. **Personalization and Adaptation:**
   - Development of generative models capable of personalizing content generation based on individual preferences, user feedback, and contextual information, leading to more tailored and adaptive AI-driven experiences.

7. **Collaborative and Interactive AI:**
   - Exploration of collaborative and interactive generative AI systems that engage users in co-creative processes, enabling human-AI collaboration to generate novel ideas, designs, or narratives.

8. **Zero-Shot and Few-Shot Learning:**
   - Research into zero-shot and few-shot learning techniques for generative models, allowing them to generalize to new tasks or domains with minimal training data, thereby improving their flexibility and adaptability.

9. **Federated and Privacy-Preserving AI:**
   - Development of federated learning and privacy-preserving techniques for generative AI, enabling model training across distributed data sources while preserving data privacy and confidentiality.

10. **Real-World Applications and Impact:**
    - Integration of generative AI technologies into various real-world applications and domains, including creative industries, entertainment, healthcare, education, and design, with a focus on delivering tangible value and positive societal impact.

Overall, the future of generative AI holds immense potential for driving innovation, creativity, and human-AI collaboration across diverse domains. By addressing emerging challenges, ethical concerns, and user needs, researchers and practitioners can shape the future of generative AI in ways that benefit society and contribute to human well-being.

Advances in Generative AI Research

Advances in generative AI research have been instrumental in pushing the boundaries of artificial intelligence, enabling machines to generate realistic and creative content across various modalities. Here are some key areas of advancement in generative AI research:

1. **Model Architectures**:
   - Development of novel model architectures, such as Generative Adversarial Networks (GANs), Variational Autoencoders (VAEs), and Transformers, which have significantly improved the quality and diversity of generated content.

   - Architectural innovations, including progressive growing techniques, attention mechanisms, and self-attention mechanisms, have enhanced the scalability, efficiency, and expressiveness of generative models.

2. **Multimodal Generation**:
   - Advancements in multimodal generative models capable of generating content across multiple modalities, including images, text, audio, and video.

   - Techniques for integrating and aligning different modalities within a single model architecture, enabling the generation of coherent and semantically meaningful multimodal content.

3. **Fine-Grained Control**:

- Techniques for fine-grained control over generated outputs, allowing users to manipulate specific attributes, styles, or characteristics of the generated content.

- Approaches such as conditional generation, style transfer, and attribute manipulation enable users to specify desired properties of the generated content with greater precision and control.

4. **Unsupervised and Self-Supervised Learning:**
   - Advances in unsupervised and self-supervised learning techniques, which enable generative models to learn from raw data without explicit supervision.

   - Self-supervised learning methods, such as contrastive learning and predictive coding, have proven effective in pretraining generative models on large-scale datasets, leading to improved performance on downstream tasks.

5. **Bias Mitigation and Fairness:**
   - Research into techniques for mitigating bias and promoting fairness in generative AI systems, addressing concerns related to algorithmic fairness, diversity, and representation.

   - Approaches for debiasing training data, regularizing model training, and enforcing fairness constraints during generation help mitigate biases and promote equitable outcomes.

6. **Interpretability and Explainability:**
   - Efforts to enhance the interpretability and explainability of generative models, enabling users to understand and interpret the underlying processes and decisions made by AI systems.

   - Techniques such as attention visualization, saliency maps, and counterfactual explanations provide insights into the inner workings of generative models and their outputs.

7. **Real-World Applications**:
    - Application of generative AI techniques in various real-world domains, including art and design, entertainment, healthcare, education, and simulation.

    - Generative models are being used to create artwork, generate music, produce synthetic data for training machine learning models, and simulate complex systems, among other applications.

Overall, advances in generative AI research have led to remarkable progress in generating realistic, diverse, and creative content across different domains, paving the way for exciting new applications and possibilities in artificial intelligence.

Challenges and Opportunities in the Field

In the field of generative AI, there exist both significant challenges and promising opportunities that shape Its research, development, and application. Let's delve into these aspects:

Challenges:

1. **Quality and Diversity of Generated Content**:
    - Ensuring the quality and diversity of generated content remains a challenge, particularly in maintaining realism and coherence across different modalities.

2. **Bias and Fairness**:
    - Addressing bias and fairness concerns in generative models, as they can perpetuate and amplify existing biases present in the training data.

3. **Interpretability and Explainability**:
    - Enhancing the interpretability and explainability of generative models, allowing users to understand and trust the decisions made by AI systems.

4. **Robustness and Generalization**:
   - Ensuring the robustness and generalization of generative models to diverse datasets and unseen scenarios, minimizing overfitting and improving performance on out-of-distribution data.

5. **Computational Complexity and Efficiency**:
   - Managing the computational complexity and resource requirements of training and deploying large-scale generative models, which can be computationally intensive and resource-intensive.

Opportunities:

1. **Creative Applications**:
   - Exploring creative applications of generative AI in art, design, music, storytelling, and entertainment, fostering innovation and pushing the boundaries of creativity.

2. **Personalization and Customization**:
   - Leveraging generative models to personalize content and experiences for individual users, enhancing user engagement and satisfaction.

3. **Simulation and Synthesis**:
   - Harnessing generative AI for simulating complex systems, synthesizing realistic data, and creating virtual environments for training and experimentation.

4. **Healthcare and Drug Discovery**:
   - Applying generative models in healthcare for medical image synthesis, drug discovery, molecular design, and personalized medicine, potentially revolutionizing healthcare research and treatment.

5. **Education and Training**:
   - Utilizing generative AI for educational purposes, such as creating interactive learning materials, generating virtual tutors, and simulating educational scenarios for immersive learning experiences.

Conclusion:

Generative AI presents both challenges and opportunities that require careful consideration and innovation. Addressing the challenges while capitalizing on the opportunities can unlock the full potential of generative AI, enabling transformative applications across diverse domains and enhancing our understanding of artificial intelligence and its impact on society.

Potential Applications and Impact on Society

Generative AI holds immense potential for a wide range of applications across various domains, with significant implications for society. Here are some potential applications and their impact:

1. Art and Creativity:
- **Art Generation**: Generative models can create stunning artwork, paintings, and digital designs, revolutionizing the art industry and inspiring new forms of creative expression.

- **Music Composition**: AI-generated music and compositions offer novel artistic experiences, enabling musicians and composers to explore new genres, styles, and sounds.

2. Language and Communication:
- **Natural Language Generation**: Generative models produce human-like text, dialogue, and narratives for conversational agents, chatbots, and virtual assistants, improving communication and interaction with AI systems.

- **Language Translation**: AI-driven translation tools facilitate cross-cultural communication by generating accurate and contextually relevant translations in real-time.

3. **Entertainment and Media:**
   - **Content Creation**: Generative AI can produce diverse content for movies, video games, virtual reality, and augmented reality, enhancing storytelling and immersive experiences.

   - **Character Design**: AI-generated characters and avatars can populate virtual worlds, video games, and animated films, enriching narratives and engaging audiences.

4. **Healthcare and Medicine:**
   - **Medical Imaging**: Generative models aid in medical image synthesis, enabling the generation of synthetic images for training machine learning algorithms and improving diagnostic accuracy.

   - **Drug Discovery**: AI-driven molecular design accelerates drug discovery processes, facilitating the development of new medications and treatments for various diseases.

4. **Education and Training:**
   - **Educational Content**: Generative AI creates interactive learning materials, virtual tutors, and educational simulations, enhancing student engagement and personalized learning experiences.

   - **Training Simulations**: Virtual environments and simulations powered by generative models enable immersive training scenarios for professionals in fields such as aviation, defense, and emergency response.

5. **Design and Engineering:**
   - **Product Design**: Generative design tools aid in product prototyping and optimization, generating innovative designs based on user requirements and constraints.

   - **Architecture and Urban Planning**: AI-driven urban planning tools create simulations and models for optimizing city layouts, infrastructure, and environmental sustainability.

6. Environmental Conservation:
- **Climate Modelling**: Generative AI models simulate climate patterns, weather forecasts, and environmental changes, aiding in climate research and policy planning.

- **Wildlife Conservation**: AI-generated data supports wildlife monitoring efforts, habitat preservation, and species conservation initiatives through predictive modeling and ecological simulations.

Conclusion:

Generative AI has the potential to transform various aspects of society, from art and entertainment to healthcare and education. By harnessing the capabilities of generative models responsibly and ethically, we can leverage AI-driven innovation to address complex challenges, improve quality of life, and shape a more inclusive and sustainable future for all.

Chapter 14 Resources and Further Reading

Here are some recommended resources and further reading materials to deepen your understanding of generative AI:

Books:

1. "Deep Learning" by Ian Goodfellow, Yoshua Bengio, and Aaron Courville
2. "Generative Deep Learning" by David Foster
3. "Deep Reinforcement Learning Hands-On" by Maxim Lapan
4. "Generative Adversarial Networks Cookbook" by Josh Kalin
5. "Natural Language Processing in Action" by Lane, Howard, and Hapke

Online Courses:

1. Coursera: "Generative Adversarial Networks (GANs) Specialization" by DeepLearning.AI
2. Udacity: "Deep Learning Nanodegree" by Udacity
3. edX: "Deep Learning Fundamentals" by Microsoft
4. Fast.ai: Practical Deep Learning for Coders

Research Papers:

1. "Generative Adversarial Nets" by Ian Goodfellow et al. (2014)
2. "Auto-Encoding Variational Bayes" by Kingma and Welling (2013)
3. "Attention Is All You Need" by Vaswani et al. (2017)
4. "Progressive Growing of GANs for Improved Quality, Stability, and Variation" by Karras et al. (2018)
5. "Generative Pre-trained Transformer 3 (GPT-3)" by Brown et al. (2020)

Websites and Blogs:
1. OpenAI Blog: https://openai.com/blog/
2. Papers with Code: https://paperswithcode.com/
3. Distill.pub: https://distill.pub/
4. Towards Data Science: https://towardsdatascience.com/

Online Communities:
1. Reddit: r/MachineLearning, r/deeplearning, r/artificial
2. Stack Overflow: https://stackoverflow.com/questions/tagged/generative-models
3. GitHub: https://github.com/topics/generative-models

Conferences and Workshops:

1. Conference on Neural Information Processing Systems (NeurIPS)
2. International Conference on Machine Learning (ICML)
3. International Conference on Learning Representations (ICLR)
4. Workshop on Generative Modeling (WGM)
5. Deep Learning Indaba: https://deeplearningindaba.com/

These resources cover a wide range of topics in generative AI, from introductory concepts to advanced research papers and practical implementations. Exploring these materials will help you stay updated on the latest developments and deepen your expertise in this rapidly evolving field.

www.ingramcontent.com/pod-product-compliance
Lightning Source LLC
Chambersburg PA
CBHW050050230526
45470CB00004B/1472